RESUMES FOR

SCIENTIFIC AND
TECHNICAL CAREERS

THIRD EDITION

RESUMES FOR

SCIENTIFIC AND TECHNICAL CAREERS

The Editors of McGraw-Hill

New York Chicago San Francisco Lisbon London Madrid Mexico City
Milan New Delhi San Juan Seoul Singapore Sydney Toronto

Library of Congress Cataloging-in-Publication Data

Resumes for scientific and technical careers / by the editors of McGraw-Hill.
— 3rd ed.
    p.   cm.
  ISBN 0-07-148219-9 (alk. paper)
    1. Scientists—Employment.   2. Engineers—Employment.   3. Resumes
(Employment).   I. McGraw-Hill Companies.

  Q147.R47   2008
  650.14'2—dc22   2007029549

1 2 3 4 5 6 7 8 9 10 11 12 13 14 15 16 17 18 19 20 21   QPD/QPD   0 9 8 7

ISBN 978-0-07-148219-6
MHID   0-07-148219-9

McGraw-Hill books are available at special quantity discounts to use as premiums and
sales promotions, or for use in corporate training programs. For more information, please
write to the Director of Special Sales, Professional Publishing, McGraw-Hill, Two Penn
Plaza, New York, NY 10121-2298. Or contact your local bookstore.

This book is printed on acid-free paper.

Contents

Introduction

Your resume is a piece of paper (or an electronic document) that serves to introduce you to the people who will eventually hire you. To write a thoughtful resume, you must thoroughly assess your personality, your accomplishments, and the skills you have acquired. The act of composing and submitting a resume also requires you to carefully consider the company or individual that might hire you. What are they looking for, and how can you meet their needs? This book shows you how to organize your personal information and experience into a concise and well-written resume, so that your qualifications and potential as an employee will be understood easily and quickly by a complete stranger.

Writing the resume is just one step in what can be a daunting job-search process, but it is an important element in the chain of events that will lead you to your new position. While you are probably a talented, bright, and charming person, your resume may not reflect these qualities. A poorly written resume can get you nowhere; a well-written resume can land you an interview and potentially a job. A good resume can even lead the interviewer to ask you questions that will allow you to talk about your strengths and highlight the skills you can bring to a prospective employer. Even a person with very little experience can find a good job if he or she is assisted by a thoughtful and polished resume.

Lengthy, typewritten resumes are a thing of the past. Today, employers do not have the time or the patience for verbose documents; they look for tightly composed, straightforward, action-based resumes. Although a one-page resume is the norm, a two-page resume may be warranted if you have had extensive job experience or have changed careers and truly need the space to properly position yourself. If, after careful editing, you still need more than one page to present yourself, it's acceptable to use a second page. A crowded resume that's hard to read would be the worst of your choices.

Distilling your work experience, education, and interests into such a small space requires preparation and thought. This book takes you step-by-step through the process of crafting an effective resume that will stand out in today's competitive marketplace. It serves as a workbook and a place to write down your experiences, while also including the techniques you'll need to pull all the necessary elements together. In the following pages, you'll find many examples of resumes that are specific to your area of interest. Study them for inspiration and find what appeals to you. There are a variety of ways to organize and present your information; inside, you'll find several that will be suitable to your needs. Good luck landing the job of your dreams!

The Elements of an Effective Resume

An effective resume is composed of information that employers are most interested in knowing about a prospective job applicant. This information is conveyed by a few essential elements. The following is a list of elements that are found in most resumes—some essential, some optional. Later in this chapter, we will further examine the role of each of these elements in the makeup of your resume.

- Heading

- Objective and/or Keyword Section

- Work Experience

- Education

- Honors

- Activities

- Certificates and Licenses

- Publications

- Professional Memberships

- Special Skills

- Personal Information

- References

The first step in preparing your resume is to gather information about yourself and your past accomplishments. Later you will refine this information, rewrite it using effective language, and organize it into an attractive layout. But first, let's take a look at each of these important elements individually so you can judge their appropriateness for your resume.

Heading

Although the heading may seem to be the simplest section of your resume, be careful not to take it lightly. It is the first section your prospective employer will see, and it contains the information she or he will need to contact you. At the very least, the heading must contain your name, your home address, and, of course, a phone number where you can be reached easily.

In today's high-tech world, many of us have multiple ways that we can be contacted. You may list your e-mail address if you are reasonably sure the employer makes use of this form of communication. Keep in mind, however, that others may have access to your e-mail messages if you send them from an account provided by your current company. If this is a concern, do not list your work e-mail address on your resume. If you are able to take calls at your current place of business, you should include your work number, because most employers will attempt to contact you during typical business hours.

If you have voice mail or a reliable answering machine at home or at work, list its number in the heading and make sure your greeting is professional and clear. Always include at least one phone number in your heading, even if it is a temporary number, where a prospective employer can leave a message.

You might have a dozen different ways to be contacted, but you do not need to list all of them. Confine your numbers or addresses to those that are the easiest for the prospective employer to use and the simplest for you to retrieve.

Objective

When seeking a specific career path, it is important to list a job or career objective on your resume. This statement helps employers know the direction you see yourself taking, so they can determine whether your goals are in line with those of their organization and the position available. Normally, an objective is one to two sentences long. Its contents will vary depending on your career field, goals, and personality. The objective can be specific or general, but it should always be to the point. See the sample resumes in this book for examples.

If you are planning to use this resume online, or you suspect your potential employer is likely to scan your resume, you will want to include a "keyword" in the objective. This allows a prospective employer, searching hundreds of resumes for a specific skill or position objective, to locate the keyword and find your resume. In essence, a keyword is what's "hot" in your particular field at a given time. It's a buzzword, a shorthand way of getting a particular message across at a glance. For example, if you are a lawyer, your objective might state your desire to work in the area of corporate litigation. In this case, someone searching for the keyword "corporate litigation" will pull up your resume and know that you want to plan, research, and present cases at trial on behalf of the corporation. If your objective states that you "desire a challenging position in systems design," the keyword is "systems design," an industry-specific shorthand way of saying that you want to be involved in assessing the need for, acquiring, and implementing high-technology systems. These are keywords and every industry has them, so it's becoming more and more important to include a few in your resume. (You may need to conduct additional research to make sure you know what keywords are most likely to be used in your desired industry, profession, or situation.)

There are many resume and job-search sites online. Like most things in the online world, they vary a great deal in quality. Use your discretion. If you plan to apply for jobs online or advertise your availability this way, you will want to design a scannable resume. This type of resume uses a format that can be easily scanned into a computer and added to a database. Scanning allows a prospective employer to use keywords to quickly review each applicant's experience and skills, and (in the event that there are many candidates for the job) to keep your resume for future reference.

Many people find that it is worthwhile to create two or more versions of their basic resume. You may want an intricately designed resume on high-quality paper to mail or hand out *and* a resume that is designed to be scanned into a computer and saved on a database or an online job site. You can even create a resume in ASCII text to e-mail to prospective employers. For further information, you may wish to refer to the *Guide to Internet Job Searching*, by Frances Roehm and Margaret Dikel, updated and published every other year by McGraw-Hill. This excellent book contains helpful and detailed information about formatting a resume for Internet use. To get you started, in Chapter 3 we have included a list of things to keep in mind when creating electronic resumes.

Although it is usually a good idea to include an objective, in some cases this element is not necessary. The goal of the objective statement is to provide the employer with an idea of where you see yourself going in the field. However, if you are uncertain of the exact nature of the job you seek, including an objective that is too specific could result in your not being considered for a host of perfectly acceptable positions. If you decide not to use an objective heading in your resume, you should definitely incorporate the information that would be conveyed in the objective into your cover letter.

Work Experience

Work experience is arguably the most important element of them all. Unless you are a recent graduate or former homemaker with little or no relevant work experience, your current and former positions will provide the central focus of the resume. You will want this section to be as complete and carefully constructed as possible. By thoroughly examining your work experience, you can get to the heart of your accomplishments and present them in a way that demonstrates and highlights your qualifications.

If you are just entering the workforce, your resume will probably focus on your education, but you should also include information on your work or volunteer experiences. Although you will have less information about work experience than a person who has held multiple positions or is advanced in his or her career, the amount of information is not what is most important in this section. How the information is presented and what it says about you as a worker and a person are what really count.

As you create this section of your resume, remember the need for accuracy. Include all the necessary information about each of your jobs, including your job title, dates of employment, name of your employer, city, state, responsibilities, special projects you handled, and accomplishments. Be sure to list only accomplishments for which you were directly responsible. And don't be alarmed if you haven't participated in or worked on special projects, because this section may not be relevant to certain jobs.

The most common way to list your work experience is in *reverse chronological order*. In other words, start with your most recent job and work your way backward. This way, your prospective employer sees your current (and often most important) position before considering your past employment. Your most recent position, if it's the most important in terms of responsibilities and relevance to the job for which you are applying, should also be the one that includes the most information as compared to your previous positions.

Even if the work itself seems unrelated to your proposed career path, you should list any job or experience that will help sell your talents. If you were promoted or given greater responsibilities or commendations, be sure to mention the fact.

The following worksheet is provided to help you organize your experiences in the working world. It will also serve as an excellent resource to refer to when updating your resume in the future.

WORK EXPERIENCE

Job One:

Job Title _____

Dates _____

Employer _____

City, State _____

Major Duties _____

_____

_____

_____

_____

_____

_____

_____

_____

_____

Special Projects _____

_____

_____

_____

Accomplishments _____

_____

_____

_____

_____

_____

Job Two:

Job Title _____

Dates _____

Employer _____

City, State _____

Major Duties _____

_____

_____

_____

_____

_____

_____

_____

Special Projects _____

_____

_____

_____

Accomplishments _____

_____

_____

_____

_____

_____

_____

_____

Job Three:

Job Title _____

Dates _____

Employer _____

City, State _____

Major Duties _____

_____

_____

_____

_____

_____

_____

Special Projects _____

_____

_____

_____

Accomplishments _____

_____

_____

_____

_____

_____

_____

_____

Job Four:

Job Title _____

Dates _____

Employer _____

City, State _____

Major Duties _____

_____

_____

_____

_____

_____

_____

_____

Special Projects _____

_____

_____

_____

Accomplishments _____

_____

_____

_____

_____

_____

_____

_____

Education

Education is usually the second most important element of a resume. Your educational background is often a deciding factor in an employer's decision to interview you. Highlight your accomplishments in school as much as you did those accomplishments at work. If you are looking for your first professional job, your education or life experience will be your greatest asset because your related work experience will be minimal. In this case, the education section becomes the most important means of selling yourself.

Include in this section all the degrees or certificates you have received; your major or area of concentration; all of the honors you earned; and any relevant activities you participated in, organized, or chaired. Again, list your most recent schooling first. If you have completed graduate-level work, begin with that and work your way back through your undergraduate education. If you have completed college, you generally should not list your high-school experience; do so only if you earned special honors, you had a grade point average that was much better than the norm, or this was your highest level of education.

If you have completed a large number of credit hours in a subject that may be relevant to the position you are seeking but did not obtain a degree, you may wish to list the hours or classes you completed. Keep in mind, however, that you may be asked to explain why you did not finish the program. If you are currently in school, list the degree, certificate, or license you expect to obtain and the projected date of completion.

The following worksheet will help you gather the information you need for this section of your resume.

EDUCATION

School One _____

Major or Area of Concentration _____

Degree _____

Dates _____

School Two _____

Major or Area of Concentration _____

Degree _____

Dates _____

Honors

If you include an honors section in your resume, you should highlight any awards, honors, or memberships in honorary societies that you have received. (You may also incorporate this information into your education section.) Often, the honors are academic in nature, but this section also may be used for special achievements in sports, clubs, or other school activities. Always include the name of the organization awarding the honor and the date(s) received. Use the following worksheet to help you gather your information.

HONORS

Honor One _____

Awarding Organization _____

Date(s) _____

Honor Two _____

Awarding Organization _____

Date(s) _____

Honor Three _____

Awarding Organization _____

Date(s) _____

Honor Four _____

Awarding Organization _____

Date(s) _____

Honor Five _____

Awarding Organization _____

Date(s) _____

Activities

Perhaps you have been active in different organizations or clubs; often an employer will look at such involvement as evidence of initiative, dedication, and good social skills. Examples of your ability to take a leading role in a group should be included on a resume, if you can provide them. The activities section of your resume should present neighborhood and community activities, volunteer positions, and so forth. In general, you may want to avoid listing any organization whose name indicates the race, creed, sex, age, marital status, sexual orientation, or nation of origin of its members because this could expose you to discrimination. Use the following worksheet to list the specifics of your activities.

ACTIVITIES

Organization/Activity _____

Accomplishments _____

_____

_____

Organization/Activity _____

Accomplishments _____

_____

_____

Organization/Activity _____

Accomplishments _____

_____

_____

As your work experience grows through the years, your school activities and honors will carry less weight and be emphasized less in your resume. Eventually, you will probably list only your degree and any major honors received. As time goes by, your job performance and the experience you've gained become the most important elements in your resume, which should change to reflect this.

Certificates and Licenses

If your chosen career path requires specialized training, you may already have certificates or licenses. You should list these if the job you are seeking requires them and you, of course, have acquired them. If you have applied for a license but have not yet received it, use the phrase "application pending."

License requirements vary by state. If you have moved or are planning to relocate to another state, check with that state's board or licensing agency for all licensing requirements.

Always make sure that all of the information you list is completely accurate. Locate copies of your certificates and licenses, and check the exact date and name of the accrediting agency. Use the following worksheet to organize the necessary information.

CERTIFICATES AND LICENSES

Name of License _____

Licensing Agency _____

Date Issued _____

Name of License _____

Licensing Agency _____

Date Issued _____

Name of License _____

Licensing Agency _____

Date Issued _____

Publications

Some professions strongly encourage or even require that you publish. If you have written, coauthored, or edited any books, articles, professional papers, or works of a similar nature that pertain to your field, you will definitely want to include this element. Remember to list the date of publication and the publisher's name, and specify whether you were the sole author or a coauthor. Book, magazine, or journal titles are generally italicized, while the titles of articles within a larger publication appear in quotes. (Check with your reference librarian for more about the appropriate way to present this information.) For scientific or research papers, you will need to give the date, place, and audience to whom the paper was presented.

Use the following worksheet to help you gather the necessary information about your publications.

PUBLICATIONS

Title and Type (Note, Article, etc.) _____

Title of Publication (Journal, Book, etc.) _____

Publisher _____

Date Published _____

Title and Type (Note, Article, etc.) _____

Title of Publication (Journal, Book, etc.) _____

Publisher _____

Date Published _____

Title and Type (Note, Article, etc.) _____

Title of Publication (Journal, Book, etc.) _____

Publisher _____

Date Published _____

Professional Memberships

Another potential element in your resume is a section listing professional memberships. Use this section to describe your involvement in professional associations, unions, and similar organizations. It is to your advantage to list any professional memberships that pertain to the job you are seeking. Many employers see your membership as representative of your desire to stay up-to-date and connected in your field. Include the dates of your involvement and whether you took part in any special activities or held any offices within the organization. Use the following worksheet to organize your information.

PROFESSIONAL MEMBERSHIPS

Name of Organization _____

Office(s) Held _____

Activities _____

Dates _____

Name of Organization _____

Office(s) Held _____

Activities _____

Dates _____

Name of Organization _____

Office(s) Held _____

Activities _____

Dates _____

Name of Organization _____

Office(s) Held _____

Activities _____

Dates _____

Special Skills

The special skills section of your resume is the place to mention any special abilities you have that relate to the job you are seeking. You can use this element to present certain talents or experiences that are not necessarily a part of your education or work experience. Common examples include fluency in a foreign language, extensive travel abroad, or knowledge of a particular computer application. "Special skills" can encompass a wide range of talents, and this section can be used creatively. However, for each skill you list, you should be able to describe how it would be a direct asset in the type of work you're seeking because employers may ask just that in an interview. If you can't think of a way to do this, it may be extraneous information.

Personal Information

Some people include personal information on their resumes. This is generally not recommended, but you might wish to include it if you think that something in your personal life, such as a hobby or talent, has some bearing on the position you are seeking. This type of information is often referred to at the beginning of an interview, when it may be used as an icebreaker. Of course, personal information regarding your age, marital status, race, religion, or sexual orientation should never appear on your resume as personal information. It should be given only in the context of memberships and activities, and only when doing so would not expose you to discrimination.

References

References are not usually given on the resume itself, but a prospective employer needs to know that you have references who may be contacted if necessary. All you need to include is a single sentence at the end of the resume: "References are available upon request," or even simply, "References available." Have a reference list ready—your interviewer may ask to see it! Contact each person on the list ahead of time to see whether it is all right for you to use him or her as a reference. This way, the person has a chance to think about what to say *before* the call occurs. This helps ensure that you will obtain the best reference possible.

Chapter 2

Writing Your Resume

Now that you have gathered the information for each section of your resume, it's time to write it out in a way that will get the attention of the reviewer—hopefully, your future employer! The language you use in your resume will affect its success, so you must be careful and conscientious. Translate the facts you have gathered into the active, precise language of resume writing. You will be aiming for a resume that keeps the reader's interest and highlights your accomplishments in a concise and effective way.

Resume writing is unlike any other form of writing. Although your seventh-grade composition teacher would not approve, the rules of punctuation and sentence building are often completely ignored. Instead, you should try for a functional, direct writing style that focuses on the use of verbs and other words that imply action on your part. Writing with action words and strong verbs characterizes you to potential employers as an energetic, active person, someone who completes tasks and achieves results from his or her work. Resumes that do not make use of action words can sound passive and stale. These resumes are not effective and do not get the attention of any employer, no matter how qualified the applicant. Choose words that display your strengths and demonstrate your initiative. The following list of commonly used verbs will help you create a strong resume:

administered	assembled
advised	assumed responsibility
analyzed	billed
arranged	built

carried out	inspected
channeled	interviewed
collected	introduced
communicated	invented
compiled	maintained
completed	managed
conducted	met with
contacted	motivated
contracted	negotiated
coordinated	operated
counseled	orchestrated
created	ordered
cut	organized
designed	oversaw
determined	performed
developed	planned
directed	prepared
dispatched	presented
distributed	produced
documented	programmed
edited	published
established	purchased
expanded	recommended
functioned as	recorded
gathered	reduced
handled	referred
hired	represented
implemented	researched
improved	reviewed

saved	supervised
screened	taught
served as	tested
served on	trained
sold	typed
suggested	wrote

Let's look at two examples that differ only in their writing style. The first resume section is ineffective because it does not use action words to accent the applicant's work experiences.

WORK EXPERIENCE
Regional Sales Manager

Manager of sales representatives from seven states. Manager of twelve food chain accounts in the East. In charge of the sales force's planned selling toward specific goals. Supervisor and trainer of new sales representatives. Consulting for customers in the areas of inventory management and quality control.

Special Projects: Coordinator and sponsor of annual Food Industry Seminar.

Accomplishments: Monthly regional volume went up 25 percent during my tenure while, at the same time, a proper sales/cost ratio was maintained. Customer-company relations were improved.

In the following paragraph, we have rewritten the same section using action words. Notice how the tone has changed. It now sounds stronger and more active. This person accomplished goals and really *did* things.

WORK EXPERIENCE
Regional Sales Manager

Managed sales representatives from seven states. Oversaw twelve food chain accounts in the eastern United States. Directed the sales force in planned selling toward specific goals. Supervised and trained new sales representatives. Counseled customers in the areas of inventory management and quality control. Coordinated and sponsored the annual Food Industry Seminar. Increased monthly regional volume by 25 percent and helped to improve customer-company relations during my tenure.

One helpful way to construct the work experience section is to make use of your actual job descriptions—the written duties and expectations your employers have for a person in your current or former position. Job descriptions are rarely written in proper resume language, so you will have to rework them, but they do include much of the information necessary to create this section of your resume. If you have access to job descriptions for your former positions, you can use the details to construct an action-oriented paragraph. Often, your human resources department can provide a job description for your current position.

The following is an example of a typical human resources job description, followed by a rewritten version of the same description employing action words and specific details about the job. Again, pay attention to the style of writing instead of the content, as the details of your own experience will be unique.

WORK EXPERIENCE
Public Administrator I

Responsibilities: Coordinate and direct public services to meet the needs of the nation, state, or community. Analyze problems; work with special committees and public agencies; recommend solutions to governing bodies.

Aptitudes and Skills: Ability to relate to and communicate with people; solve complex problems through analysis; plan, organize, and implement policies and programs. Knowledge of political systems, financial management, personnel administration, program evaluation, and organizational theory.

WORK EXPERIENCE
Public Administrator I

Wrote pamphlets and conducted discussion groups to inform citizens of legislative processes and consumer issues. Organized and supervised 25 interviewers. Trained interviewers in effective communication skills.

After you have written out your resume, you are ready to begin the next important step: assembly and layout.

Chapter 3

Assembly and Layout

At this point, you've gathered all the necessary information for your resume and rewritten it in language that will impress your potential employers. Your next step is to assemble the sections in a logical order and lay them out on the page neatly and attractively to achieve the desired effect: getting the interview.

Assembly

The order of the elements in a resume makes a difference in its overall effect. Clearly, you would not want to bury your name and address somewhere in the middle of the resume. Nor would you want to lead with a less important section, such as special skills. Put the elements in an order that stresses your most important accomplishments and the things that will be most appealing to your potential employer. For example, if you are new to the workforce, you will want the reviewer to read about your education and life skills before any part-time jobs you may have held for short durations. On the other hand, if you have been gainfully employed for several years and currently hold an important position in your company, you should list your work accomplishments ahead of your educational information, which has become less pertinent with time.

Certain things should always be included in your resume, but others are optional. The following list shows you which are which. You might want to use it as a checklist to be certain that you have included all of the necessary information.

Essential	**Optional**
Name	Cellular Phone Number
Address	Pager Number
Phone Number	E-Mail Address or Website Address
Work Experience	Voice Mail Number
Education	Job Objective
References Phrase	Honors
	Special Skills
	Publications
	Professional Memberships
	Activities
	Certificates and Licenses
	Personal Information
	Graphics
	Photograph

Your choice of optional sections depends on your own background and employment needs. Always use information that will put you in a favorable light—unless it's absolutely essential, avoid anything that will prompt the interviewer to ask questions about your weaknesses or something else that could be unflattering. Make sure your information is accurate and truthful. If your honors are impressive, include them in the resume. If your activities in school demonstrate talents that are necessary for the job you are seeking, allow space for a section on activities. If you are applying for a position that requires ornamental illustration, you may want to include border illustrations or graphics that demonstrate your talents in this area. If you are answering an advertisement for a job that requires certain physical traits, a photo of yourself might be appropriate. A person applying for a job as a computer programmer would *not* include a photo as part of his or her resume. Each resume is unique, just as each person is unique.

Types of Resumes

So far we have focused on the most common type of resume—the *reverse chronological* resume—in which your most recent job is listed first. This is the type of resume usually preferred by those who have to read a large number of resumes, and it is by far the most popular and widely circulated. However, this style of presentation may not be the most effective way to highlight *your* skills and accomplishments.

For example, if you are reentering the workforce after many years or are trying to change career fields, the *functional* resume may work best. This type of resume puts the focus on your achievements instead of the sequence of your work history. In the functional resume, your experience is presented through your general accomplishments and the skills you have developed in your working life.

A functional resume is assembled from the same information you gathered in Chapter 1. The main difference lies in how you organize the information. Essentially, the work experience section is divided in two, with your job duties and accomplishments constituting one section and your employers' names, cities, and states; your positions; and the dates employed making up the other. Place the first section near the top of your resume, just below your job objective (if used), and call it *Accomplishments* or *Achievements*. The second section, containing the bare essentials of your work history, should come after the accomplishments section and can be called *Employment History*, since it is a chronological overview of your former jobs.

The other sections of your resume remain the same. The work experience section is the only one affected in the functional format. By placing the section that focuses on your achievements at the beginning, you draw attention to these achievements. This puts less emphasis on where you worked and when, and more on what you did and what you are capable of doing.

If you are changing careers, the emphasis on skills and achievements is important. The identities of previous employers (who aren't part of your new career field) need to be downplayed. A functional resume can help accomplish this task. If you are reentering the workforce after a long absence, a functional resume is the obvious choice. And if you lack full-time work experience, you will need to draw attention away from this fact and put the focus on your skills and abilities. You may need to highlight your volunteer activities and part-time work. Education may also play a more important role in your resume.

The type of resume that is right for you will depend on your personal circumstances. It may be helpful to create both types and then compare them. Which one presents you in the best light? Examples of both types of resumes are included in this book. Use the sample resumes in Chapter 5 to help you decide on the content, presentation, and look of your own resume.

Resume or Curriculum Vitae?

A curriculum vitae (CV) is a longer, more detailed synopsis of your professional history that generally runs three or more pages in length. It includes a summary of your educational and academic background as well as teaching and research experience, publications, presentations, awards, honors, affiliations, and other details. Because the purpose of the CV is different from that of the resume, many of the rules we've discussed thus far involving style and length do not apply.

A curriculum vitae is used primarily for admissions applications to graduate or professional schools, independent consulting in a variety of settings, proposals for fellowships or grants, or applications for positions in academia. As with a resume, you may need different versions of a CV for different types of positions. You should only send a CV when one is specifically requested by an employer or institution.

Like a resume, your CV should include your name, contact information, education, skills, and experience. In addition to the basics, a CV includes research and teaching experience, publications, grants and fellowships, professional associations and licenses, awards, and other information relevant to the position for which you are applying. You can follow the advice presented thus far to gather and organize your personal information.

Special Tips for Electronic Resumes

Because there are many details to consider in writing a resume that will be posted or transmitted on the Internet, or one that will be scanned into a computer when it is received, we suggest that you refer to the *Guide to Internet Job Searching*, by Frances Roehm and Margaret Dikel, as previously mentioned. However, here are some brief, general guidelines to follow if you expect your resume to be scanned into a computer.

- Use standard fonts in which none of the letters touch.

- Keep in mind that underlining, italics, and fancy scripts may not scan well.

- Use boldface and capitalization to set off elements. Again, make sure letters don't touch. Leave at least a quarter inch between lines of type.

- Keep information and elements at the left margin. Centering, columns, and even indenting may change when the resume is optically scanned.

- Do not use any lines, boxes, or graphics.

- Place the most important information at the top of the first page. If you use two pages, put "Page 1 of 2" at the bottom of the first page and put your name and "Page 2 of 2" at the top of the second page.

- List each telephone number on its own line in the header.

- Use multiple keywords or synonyms for what you do to make sure your qualifications will be picked up if a prospective employer is searching for them. Use nouns that are keywords for your profession.

- Be descriptive in your titles. For example, don't just use "assistant"; use "legal office assistant."

- Make sure the contrast between print and paper is good. Use a high-quality laser printer and white or very light colored 8½-by-11-inch paper.

- Mail a high-quality laser print or an excellent copy. Do not fold or use staples, as this might interfere with scanning. You may, however, use paper clips.

In addition to creating a resume that works well for scanning, you may want to have a resume that can be e-mailed to reviewers. Because you may not know what word processing application the recipient uses, the best format to use is ASCII text. (ASCII stands for "American Standard Code for Information Interchange.") It allows people with very different software platforms to exchange and understand information. (E-mail operates on this principle.) ASCII is a simple, text-only language, which means you can include only simple text. There can be no use of boldface, italics, or even paragraph indentations.

To create an ASCII resume, just use your normal word processing program; when finished, save it as a "text only" document. You will find this option under the "save" or "save as" command. Here is a list of things to *avoid* when crafting your electronic resume:

- Tabs. Use your space bar. Tabs will not work.

- Any special characters, such as mathematical symbols.

- Word wrap. Use hard returns (the return key) to make line breaks.

- Centering or other formatting. Align everything at the left margin.

- Bold or italic fonts. Everything will be converted to plain text when you save the file as a "text only" document.

Check carefully for any mistakes before you save the document as a text file. Spellcheck and proofread it several times; then ask someone with a keen eye to go over it again for you. Remember: the key is to keep it simple. Any attempt to make this resume pretty or decorative may result in a resume that is confusing and hard to read. After you have saved the document, you can cut and paste it into an e-mail or onto a website.

Layout for a Paper Resume

A great deal of care—and much more formatting—is necessary to achieve an attractive layout for your paper resume. There is no single appropriate layout that applies to every resume, but there are a few basic rules to follow in putting your resume on paper:

- Leave a comfortable margin on the sides, top, and bottom of the page (usually one to one and a half inches).

- Use appropriate spacing between the sections (two to three line spaces are usually adequate).

- Be consistent in the *type* of headings you use for different sections of your resume. For example, if you capitalize the heading EMPLOYMENT HISTORY, don't use initial capitals and underlining for a section of equal importance, such as Education.

- Do not use more than one font in your resume. Stay consistent by choosing a font that is fairly standard and easy to read, and don't change it for different sections. Beware of the tendency to try to make your resume original by choosing fancy type styles; your resume may end up looking unprofessional instead of creative. Unless you are in a very creative and artistic field, you should almost always stick with tried-and-true type styles like Times New Roman and Palatino, which are often used in business writing. In the area of resume styles, conservative is usually the best way to go.

CHRONOLOGICAL RESUME

Michael S. Flowers

4459 Palm Drive
Las Vegas, NV 89154
M.Flowers@xxx.com
(702) 555-8666

EDUCATION

1965–1966	University of Nevada, Reno, NV. Business Administration Major.
1967–1968	Truckee Meadows Community College, Truckee, NV. Math Major.
1968–1973	International Business School, Civil Engineering Certificate.
1991–1993	University of Southern California, Los Angeles, CA. Master of Business Administration.

EXPERIENCE

Desert Construction, Inc., Las Vegas, NV
9/98–Present, Manager of Estimating and Engineering

Oversee and manage all estimating and engineering.

L. A. Smith Construction Company, San Diego, CA
4/95–9/98, Manager of Estimating and Engineering, Heavy/Marine Division

Supervise division engineer and estimating manager for heavy and marine estimating and construction. Market segments are heavy engineering, northeast transit, and hazardous waste work.

Brownell Corporation, Long Beach, CA
11/89–3/95, Vice-President/Manager of Heavy Estimating

Established joint venture procedures. Arranged complete estimates for joint ventures. Supervised estimators in estimating and bidding projects such as treatment plants, power plants, airport terminals, piers and docks, pumping plants, subways, and mass transit. Upgraded computer format for heavy estimating.

Flowers Consulting, Los Angeles, CA
5/86–11/87, President

Formed company to provide consulting services. Advised Southern California Water District in reconstructing a CPM schedule of a water treatment plant.

References Available Upon Request

FUNCTIONAL RESUME

WILLIAM J. SHAW

1810 Cedar Crest Blvd.
Lacy, WA 98503
Bill.Shaw@xxx.com
(360) 555-1479

CAREER SUMMARY

More than twenty years' experience in manufacturing, production, and assembly of medium- and high-volume stamping and fabrication operations. Supervised activities in fabrication, stamping, welding, and finishing of automotive and agricultural equipment as well as appliances. Responsible for training, scheduling, safety, work quality, material movement, and discipline.

TECHNICAL QUALIFICATIONS

Experienced with JIT, MRP, statistical process control, and automated visual inventory/scheduling concepts. Proficient in high-speed light stampings, transfer press operations, heavy stamped assemblies, welding, and testing instrumentation/procedures.

EMPLOYMENT HISTORY

Whirlpool Corporation, Seattle, WA   *8/00 to present*
Operations/Finishing Manager

Ford Motor Company, San Leandro, CA   *6/87 to 8/00*
Positions held: Supervisor of Cab Fabrication/Finishing, Maintenance Supervisor, and Finished Vehicle Assembly Supervisor

EDUCATION

B.S. in Business Administration, Carnegie Mellon University, 1986

References available on request

- Always try to fit your resume on one page. If you are having trouble with this, you may be trying to say too much. Edit out any repetitive or unnecessary information, and shorten descriptions of earlier jobs where possible. Ask a friend you trust for feedback on what seems unnecessary or unimportant. For example, you may have included too many optional sections. Today, with the prevalence of the personal computer as a tool, there is no excuse for a poorly laid out resume. Experiment with variations until you are pleased with the result.

Remember that a resume is not an autobiography. Too much information will only get in the way. The more compact your resume, the easier it will be to review. If a person who is swamped with resumes looks at yours, catches the main points, and then calls you for an interview to fill in some of the details, your resume has already accomplished its task. A clear and concise resume makes for a happy reader and a good impression.

There are times when, despite extensive editing, the resume simply cannot fit on one page. In this case, the resume should be laid out on two pages in such a way that neither clarity nor appearance is compromised. Each page of a two-page resume should be marked clearly: the first should indicate "Page 1 of 2," and the second should include your name and the page number, for example, "Julia Ramirez—Page 2 of 2." The pages should then be paper-clipped together. You may use a smaller type size (in the same font as the body of your resume) for the page numbers. Place them at the bottom of page one and the top of page two. Again, spend the time now to experiment with the layout until you find one that looks good to you.

Always show your final layout to other people and ask them what they like or dislike about it, and what impresses them most when they read your resume. Make sure that their responses are the same as what you want to elicit from your prospective employer. If they aren't the same, you should continue to make changes until the necessary information is emphasized.

Proofreading

After you have finished typing the master copy of your resume and before you have it copied or printed, thoroughly check it for typing and spelling errors. Do not place all your trust in your computer's spellcheck function. Use an old editing trick and read the whole resume backward—start at the end and read it right to left and bottom to top. This can help you see the small errors or inconsistencies that are easy to overlook. Take time to do it right because a single error on a document this important can cause the reader to judge your attention to detail in a harsh light.

Have several people look at the finished resume just in case you've missed an error. Don't try to take a shortcut; not having an unbiased set of eyes examine your resume now could mean embarrassment later. Even experienced editors can easily overlook their own errors. Be thorough and conscientious with your proofreading so your first impression is a perfect one.

We have included the following rules of capitalization and punctuation to assist you in the final stage of creating your resume. Remember that resumes often require use of a shorthand style of writing that may include sentences without periods and other stylistic choices that break the standard rules of grammar. Be consistent in each section and throughout the whole resume with your choices.

RULES OF CAPITALIZATION

- Capitalize proper nouns, such as names of schools, colleges, and universities; names of companies; and brand names of products.

- Capitalize major words in the names and titles of books, tests, and articles that appear in the body of your resume.

- Capitalize words in major section headings of your resume.

- Do not capitalize words just because they seem important.

- When in doubt, consult a style manual such as *Words into Type* (Prentice Hall) or *The Chicago Manual of Style* (The University of Chicago Press). Your local library can help you locate these and other reference books. Many computer programs also have grammar help sections.

RULES OF PUNCTUATION

- Use commas to separate words in a series.

- Use a semicolon to separate series of words that already include commas within the series. (For an example, see the first rule of capitalization.)

- Use a semicolon to separate independent clauses that are not joined by a conjunction.

- Use a period to end a sentence.

- Use a colon to show that examples or details follow that will expand or amplify the preceding phrase.

- Avoid the use of dashes.

- Avoid the use of brackets.

- If you use any punctuation in an unusual way in your resume, be consistent in its use.

- Whenever you are uncertain, consult a style manual.

Putting Your Resume in Print

You will need to buy high-quality paper for your printer before you print your finished resume. Regular office paper is not good enough for resumes; the reviewer will probably think it looks flimsy and cheap. Go to an office supply store or copy shop and select a high-quality bond paper that will make a good first impression. Select colors like white, off-white, or possibly a light gray. In some industries, a pastel may be acceptable, but be sure the color and feel of the paper make a subtle, positive statement about you. Nothing in the choice of paper should be loud or unprofessional.

If your computer printer does not reproduce your resume properly and produces smudged or stuttered type, either ask to borrow a friend's or take your disk (or a clean original) to a printer or copy shop for high-quality copying. If you anticipate needing a large number of copies, taking your resume to a copy shop or a printer is probably the best choice.

Hold a sheet of your unprinted bond paper up to the light. If it has a watermark, you will want to point this out to the person helping you with copies; the printing should be done so that the reader can read the print and see the watermark the right way up. Check each copy for smudges or streaks. This is the time to be a perfectionist—the results of your careful preparation will be well worth it.

The Cover Letter

Once your resume has been assembled, laid out, and printed to your satisfaction, the next and final step before distribution is to write your cover letter. Though there may be instances where you deliver your resume in person, you will usually send it through the mail or online. Resumes sent through the mail always need an accompanying letter that briefly introduces you and your resume. The purpose of the cover letter is to get a potential employer to read your resume, just as the purpose of the resume is to get that same potential employer to call you for an interview.

Like your resume, your cover letter should be clean, neat, and direct. A cover letter usually includes the following information:

1. Your name and address (unless it already appears on your personal letterhead) and your phone number(s); see item 7.

2. The date.

3. The name and address of the person and company to whom you are sending your resume.

4. The salutation ("Dear Mr." or "Dear Ms." followed by the person's last name, or "To Whom It May Concern" if you are answering a blind ad).

5. An opening paragraph explaining why you are writing (for example, in response to an ad, as a follow-up to a previous meeting, at the suggestion of someone you both know) and indicating that you are interested in whatever job is being offered.

6. One or more paragraphs that tell why you want to work for the company and what qualifications and experiences you can bring to the position. This is a good place to mention some detail about

that particular company that makes you want to work for them; this shows that you have done some research before applying.

7. A final paragraph that closes the letter and invites the reviewer to contact you for an interview. This can be a good place to tell the potential employer which method would be best to use when contacting you. Be sure to give the correct phone number and a good time to reach you, if that is important. You may mention here that your references are available upon request.

8. The closing ("Sincerely" or "Yours truly") followed by your signature in a dark ink, with your name typed under it.

Your cover letter should include all of this information and be no longer than one page in length. The language used should be polite, businesslike, and to the point. Don't attempt to tell your life story in the cover letter; a long and cluttered letter will serve only to annoy the reader. Remember that you need to mention only a few of your accomplishments and skills in the cover letter. The rest of your information is available in your resume. If your cover letter is a success, your resume will be read and all pertinent information reviewed by your prospective employer.

Producing the Cover Letter

Cover letters should always be individualized because they are always written to specific individuals and companies. Never use a form letter for your cover letter or copy it as you would a resume. Each cover letter should be unique, and as personal and lively as possible. (Of course, once you have written and rewritten your first cover letter until you are satisfied with it, you can certainly use similar wording in subsequent letters. You may want to save a template on your computer for future reference.) Keep a hard copy of each cover letter so you know exactly what you wrote in each one.

There are sample cover letters in Chapter 6. Use them as models or for ideas of how to assemble and lay out your own cover letters. Remember that every letter is unique and depends on the particular circumstances of the individual writing it and the job for which he or she is applying.

After you have written your cover letter, proofread it as thoroughly as you did your resume. Again, spelling or punctuation errors are a sure sign of carelessness, and you don't want that to be a part of your first impression on a prospective employer. This is no time to trust your spellcheck function. Even after going through a spelling and grammar check, your cover letter should be carefully proofread by at least one other person.

Print the cover letter on the same quality bond paper you used for your resume. Remember to sign it, using a good dark-ink pen. Handle the letter and resume carefully to avoid smudging or wrinkling, and mail them together in an appropriately sized envelope. Many stores sell matching envelopes to coordinate with your choice of bond paper.

Keep an accurate record of all resumes you send out and the results of each mailing. This record can be kept on your computer, in a calendar or notebook, or on file cards. Knowing when a resume is likely to have been received will keep you on track as you make follow-up phone calls.

About a week after mailing resumes and cover letters to potential employers, contact them by telephone. Confirm that your resume arrived and ask whether an interview might be possible. Be sure to record the name of the person you spoke to and any other information you gleaned from the conversation. It is wise to treat the person answering the phone with a great deal of respect; sometimes the assistant or receptionist has the ear of the person doing the hiring.

You should make a great impression with the strong, straightforward resume and personalized cover letter you have just created. We wish you every success in securing the career of your dreams!

Chapter 5

Sample Resumes

This chapter contains dozens of sample resumes for people pursuing a wide variety of jobs and careers in scientific and technical fields.

There are many different styles of resumes in terms of graphic layout and presentation of information. These samples represent people with varying amounts of education and experience. Use them as models for your own resume. Choose one resume or borrow elements from several different resumes to help you construct your own.

Jason Alexander

345 East 82nd Street • New York, NY 10028 • jason.alexander@xxx.com
Cell: (212) 555-3654 • Home: (212) 555-9065

OBJECTIVE

Senior MIS management position in an international firm with long-range personal growth potential.

SUMMARY

Fifteen years of MIS experience in developing large-scale commercial systems. Solid technical background in multi-language programming and system design with extensive user interfacing. Held increasingly important MIS management positions over the last ten years.

EDUCATION

Cornell University, B.S., Mathematics (1988), M.A., Statistics (1992)

TECHNICAL

Equipment: IBM, DOS/VSE, OS/MVS, CICS, TSO/ROSCOE, SPERRY, DMS/TIP

Languages: MySql, C++, COBOL, FORTRAN, INQUIRE, MARK IV, RPG, SMP

EXPERIENCE

2003 - Present   DELOITTE & TOUCHE, NEW YORK, NEW YORK

Assistant MIS Director, Systems & Programming (2005 - Present)

- Direct a systems and programming organization of 40 MIS professionals in the development and enhancement of the firm's internal business system.

- Oversee major developments in the areas of client management, general ledger, accounts receivable, personnel, and partnership accounting.

Manager, MIS Applications Development (2003 - 2005)

- Staffed and directed a Systems & Programming group of 20 MIS professionals in the design and development of a firm-wide online database to maintain the firm's client base and to track the professional consulting staff's time and expenses.

- Directed project definition and functional analysis phase of project life cycle.

- Recruited 10 full-time analysts and programmers to develop detailed systems design and specifications using top-down structured methodology.

- Coordinated the design and development of a complex database structure to support the online informational needs of the firm.

- Initiated the development of naming standards, program skeletons, reusable code, and macro routines to assist and standardize the program construction phase of development.
- Developed and instituted a base case testing methodology for the comprehensive testing and quality assurance of the developed system.

1993 - 2003   IBM CORPORATION, WHITE PLAINS, NEW YORK

Manager, MIS Development Projects (2001 - 2003)

- Coordinated migration and implementation of financial and administrative systems being developed by European operations for use in the Latin American affiliates.
- Defined and implemented migration strategy and procedure for all MIS activities, including software, testing, and affiliate training.
- Conceived, designed, and negotiated first-time maintenance and emergency procedures for ongoing production support between European development center and Latin American affiliates.
- Initiated, developed, and implemented online strategy on optimum cost-effective general guidelines and procedures for all CICS applications in Latin America.

Manager, Systems Projects (1996 - 2001)

- Developed and managed increasingly complex systems culminating in the direction of two-year retail finance and leasing system.
- Directed and implemented front-end CICS system that reduced input from ten to three days.
- Expanded and revamped existing system to mechanize all edits/validations and provide timely management reporting.
- Directed systems and programming staff of eight in development/maintenance of systems in areas of supply/service billing, equipment control, collection services, insurance loss, and vehicle asset tracking.
- Conceived, directed, and implemented modularized table system.
- Instituted block system releases resulting in greater throughput of user requests and reduced direct overhead costs.

Senior Programming Consultant (1993 - 1996)

- Project leader of five systems and programming personnel in maintenance and enhancement of monthly equipment billing system.
- Organized function to support end users of marketing, finance, and service/distribution in developing their own inquiries for management information.

References available on request

PABLO SANCHEZ

500 Briar Patch Rd.
Frankfort, KY 40601
(502) 555-8750
P.Sanchez@xxx.com

OBJECTIVE

Foreman or heavy equipment operator

PROFESSIONAL EXPERIENCE

From June 2005 to present
Scraper Superintendent, Kentucky Department of Transportation
- Involved in extensive training program initiated by state to give hands-on training to operators and mechanical staff on Cat models 631E, D10N, and 16G
- Trained operators in the loading sequence by utilizing the chain loading method
- Supervised and directed scraper fleet on a daily basis
- Supervised and operated dozer on earth-fill dam project
- Operated truck fleet on overburden removal in a gold mine

From July 2000 to January 2005
Owner and operator of trucking/construction company, Sanchez Construction
- Worked on small- to medium-sized construction projects for private sector as well as Soil Conservation Service and U.S. Army Corps of Engineers
- Assistant Quality Control official for Soil Conservation Service and U.S. Army Corps of Engineers on flood cleanup
- Instituted my own maintenance program and did most of the mechanical work
- Trucking for such contractors as Mason Corp., Daniel Industries, SJ Almaden, PB Snyder, Kentucky Excavating, Anton Construction, Hugh Bowman Contracting, and Landfill Crossroads, Inc.

EQUIPMENT SKILLS

From 1996 to 2000

Caterpillar:	Dozers, Loaders, Scrapers, Excavators
Komatsu:	Dozers, Excavators
Clark:	Excavators
John Deere:	Excavators
Holland:	Belt Loaders

EDUCATION

Mason County Joint Vocational School

Diesel Mechanics and Welding

Graduated 1995

MEMBERSHIPS

Fraternal Order of Elks

Fraternal Order of Police, Lodge #55

International Union of Operating Engineers, Local 555, Frankfort, Kentucky

REFERENCES

Available upon request

Mark F. Fulton

Mark.Fulton@xxx.com

Current Address: Permanent Address:
78 Prairie Road   26 Frenwood Road
Columbus, Ohio 43216   Steubenville, Ohio 40605
(614) 555-3981   (614) 555-1807

OBJECTIVE

To obtain a position in construction engineering and management.

EDUCATION

Ohio State University, Columbus, Ohio
Master of Science, Civil Engineering
Graduated May 2006

University of Dayton, Dayton, Ohio
Bachelor of Engineering, Civil Engineering
Graduated Cum Laude, May 2005

HONORS

Regents Fellowship, Ohio State University
Harry Long Memorial Prize, University of Dayton
Dean's List for six semesters, University of Dayton

EXPERIENCE

Summer 2004

Ohio Department of Transportation, Steubenville, Ohio
Engineer in Training
Worked with Resident Engineer's office. Responsible for inspecting the construction of a reinforced concrete bridge and roadway. Made daily reports and kept detailed records of contractor performance and progress.

Summer 2003

Hayes, Jones, and Bowers, Steubenville, Ohio
Engineering Aide
Worked with professional engineers in the design of roadways and structures. Responsible for hydrologic aspects of highway design. Participated on in-depth bridge inspection.

Page 1 of 2

EXPERIENCE (*cont.*)

Summer 2002

Hayes, Jones, and Bowers, Steubenville, Ohio
Engineering Aide
Worked with professional engineers in design of wastewater treatment plants and sewer systems. Responsible for AutoCAD drawings and checking design calculations.

CERTIFICATION

Passed the April 2006 Engineer in Training exam.

REFERENCES

Professor B. William Gebbs
Ohio State University
80 Lawrence Hall
Columbus, Ohio 43210
B.Gebbs@xxx.com

Professor Roger K. Hadley
University of Dayton
P.O. Box 8020-C
Dayton, Ohio 45469
Roger.Hadley@xxx.com

PATRICIA GOLDBERG

1480 Dean Road ■ Sacramento, CA 95819 ■ Patty.Goldberg@xxx.com ■ (916) 555-9306

OBJECTIVE:

A challenging and rewarding position in the environmental field.

EDUCATION:

Bachelor of Science, University of California at San Diego, 1997
Aquatic Biology, Minor in Natural Resources

EXPERIENCE:

CALIFORNIA DEPARTMENT OF ENVIRONMENTAL MANAGEMENT, Sacramento, CA

March 2004 - Present
Environmental Project Manager, State Cleanup Section, Environmental Response.

- Manage the cleanup of hazardous waste sites.
- Contract the disposal of hazardous materials.
- Negotiate cleanup issues with PRPs.
- Conduct field sampling and contractor overview.

July 2003 - March 2004
Environmental Manager, Facilities Planning Section, Water Management.

- Implemented outreach program for building of treatment facilities in small communities.
- Performed primary and secondary review of facilities-planning documents for the construction grants program.
- Interfaced with engineering firms and evaluated project costs.

April 1999 - June 2003
Environmental Scientist, Permits Section, Water Management.

- Reviewed program documents and managed implementation of municipal programs.
- Aided in the implementation of the state pretreatment program.
- Wrote permits for industrial users, NPDES, and land application.
- Conducted audits of municipal pretreatment programs and inspected manufacturing facilities.

Page 1 of 2

EXPERIENCE *(continued):*

LAKE SHASTA RECREATION AREA, Shasta, CA

April 1998 - September 1998
Park Naturalist.

- Managed the activities of park nature center.
- Conducted environmental programs for park visitors.

AFFILIATIONS:

Institutes of Hazardous Materials Management.

National Wildlife Federation.

Water Pollution Control Federation.

REFERENCES:

Available upon request.

Tony Sabatini

Present Address	Permanent Address
450 West Pontiac Lane	1929 Ford Drive
East Lansing, Michigan 48824	Detroit, Michigan 48183
(517) 555-6534	(313) 555-4631

Objective

Obtain engineering employment involving design and construction of roads, bridges, and associated structures

Experience

Senior Class Project: Design of Concrete Slab Road Test Facility

Spring 2006
Appleby, Inc., Detroit, Michigan
Skilled Laborer/Supervisor
Site surveys and layouts, excavation, concrete placement and finishing, plumbing, carpentry, and equipment operation

Summers 2003 - 2005
Lowell Construction, Detroit, Michigan
General Laborer
Concrete placement and finishing, carpentry, and excavation

Holiday Season, 2003
Sales Representative
L. D. Jones and Sons, East Lansing, Michigan

Education

Michigan State University, May 2006
Bachelor of Science in Civil Engineering
Dean's List, 2003 - 2004

University of Michigan, June 2004
Major - Electrical Engineering
Dean's List, 2003

Certified Engineer in Training, June 2006

Michael S. Flowers

4459 Palm Drive
Las Vegas, NV 89154
M.Flowers@xxx.com
(702) 555-8666

EDUCATION

1965–1966	University of Nevada, Reno, NV. Business Administration Major.
1967–1968	Truckee Meadows Community College, Truckee, NV. Math Major.
1968–1973	International Business School, Civil Engineering Certificate.
1991–1993	University of Southern California, Los Angeles, CA. Master of Business Administration.

EXPERIENCE

Desert Construction, Inc., Las Vegas, NV
9/98–Present, Manager of Estimating and Engineering

Oversee and manage all estimating and engineering.

L. A. Smith Construction Company, San Diego, CA
4/95–9/98, Manager of Estimating and Engineering, Heavy/Marine Division

Supervise division engineer and estimating manager for heavy and marine estimating and construction. Market segments are heavy engineering, northeast transit, and hazardous waste work.

Brownell Corporation, Long Beach, CA
11/89–3/95, Vice-President/Manager of Heavy Estimating

Established joint venture procedures. Arranged complete estimates for joint ventures. Supervised estimators in estimating and bidding projects such as treatment plants, power plants, airport terminals, piers and docks, pumping plants, subways, and mass transit. Upgraded computer format for heavy estimating.

Flowers Consulting, Los Angeles, CA
5/86–11/87, President

Formed company to provide consulting services. Advised Southern California Water District in reconstructing a CPM schedule of a water treatment plant.

References Available Upon Request

JOHN K. LAI

20 West Concord Street   Dover, NH 03820   John.Lai@xxx.com   (603) 555-1703

EDUCATION

B.S., Civil Engineering, University of New Hampshire

CAREER SUMMARY

Extensive experience in program management on complex construction projects. Managed all phases of project administration, contract development, and claims negotiation. Proven knowledge and skills; ability to interact with professionals, contractors, and labor personnel.

EXPERIENCE

2004–Present, Johnson, Incorporated
Position: Resident Engineer, North Shore Interceptor, Phase IV
Location: Concord, New Hampshire

Duties: Supervise performance of construction contractors. Project includes tunnels, deep shafts, chambers, odor control structures, and appurtenant facilities.

2003–2004, Bechtel
Position: Project Manager
Location: Hanford, Washington

Duties: Special consultant to the Department of Energy and Rockwell International for design and construction of underground and shaft facilities for storage of nuclear waste.

2001–2003, Bechtel
Position: Project Manager, Construction Services
Location: Los Angeles, California

Duties: Prepared division budgets, long-range plans, and project proposals. Assigned construction personnel to projects. Acted as area construction manager on the proposal for Los Angeles Subway Construction. Supervised preparation of procedures for construction of power generation plant and coal mine in China.

REGISTRATION

Registered to work in New Hampshire

Page 1 of 2

AFFILIATIONS

American Management Association

Society of American Military Engineers

Society of Mining Engineers

REFERENCES

Available upon request

KAREN S. ADAMS

1685 Mountain Road • Tucson, AZ 85720 • Karen.Adams@xxx.com • (602) 555-8960

PROJECT MANAGEMENT

Project management for medium-sized company. Working toward international construction management with an eye on environmental compatibility.

PROFESSIONAL EXPERIENCE

2004–Present

University of Arizona Physical Plant, Tucson, AZ
Position: Project Coordinator
Responsibilities include:

- Start-to-finish management of construction projects
- Estimating, assembling technical teams, surveying and layout, some design/drafting/autoCAD, specs, job supervision, and inspection
- Redesign of local problem intersection

Prior to 2004

Thirteen years in the construction industry, starting as a laborer in 1988, ending as a journeyman, formsetter, and concrete finisher. Experience as crew supervisor, tractor operator, job supervisor, and estimator.

STRENGTHS AND CAPABILITIES

- Detail- and big picture–orientation
- Anticipating and solving problems
- Very good with numbers in the field and with people
- Bringing projects in on time and within budget without sacrificing quality

ACADEMIC BACKGROUND

1996–2000

Senior in Civil Engineering at the University of Arizona, Tucson, AZ

- G.P.A. of 3.85
- Outstanding Junior and Outstanding Service Awards for 1999
- Honors recipient every year between 1997 and 2000
- Coursework stressing construction management and environmental and geotechnical engineering
- Graduated May 2000

Josh C. Hassan

655 Kelton Ave. ◆ Denver, CO 80010 ◆ (303) 555-7300
j.hassan@xxx.com

◆ OBJECTIVE

A position that will utilize my academic background and experience in outside industrial sales

◆ EDUCATIONAL BACKGROUND

1996 – 2000: Bachelor of Commerce

University of Windsor, Windsor, Ontario

Concentrating in marketing, finance, and accounting

◆ PROFESSIONAL EXPERIENCE

April 2002 – present: Sales Engineer/Outside Sales Representative

Washington Electric, Dayton, OH

Responsible for outside sales of special machinery and project coordinator in the southeastern Michigan, Ohio, and Ontario areas. Launch and follow progress of machines from design to testing. Act as liaison between client/customer and plant. Assist in pricing and custom design of all machines. Develop and design brochures as selling tool. Continuously search for new and innovative techniques to reach the company's specific market. Deal predominantly with the auto, food, heating, and cooling industries.

◆ SPECIAL SKILLS

Strong working knowledge of Microsoft Office, including Word, PowerPoint and Excel

Comfortable making cold calls

Very familiar with the automotive market and related industries

◆ REFERENCES

Available upon request

Vajid L. Singh

P.O. Box 1296
Stanford, CA 94309
Singh@xxx.com
(415) 555-0701

EDUCATION

Master of Business Administration, June 2006
Stanford University, Stanford, CA

Bachelor of Technology, Civil Engineering, July 2000
Institute of Technology, New Delhi, India

EMPLOYMENT

Field Engineer, August 2000 to July 2004
Nardini Co., Ltd. (subsidiary of Ferguson Construction, Inc., United Kingdom)
New Delhi, India

- Managed construction sites as independent profit centers consistently achieving target margins
- Supervised and directed work of four supervisors and 25 skilled workers
- Prepared cost estimates and quantity surveys for contract bids and analyzed project proposals
- Collected, analyzed, and interpreted data pertaining to financial and production performance of site; wrote reports to facilitate control
- Negotiated on a regular basis with labor unions and clients

Graduate Teaching Assistant, September 2004 to June 2006
Stanford University, Stanford, CA

- Graded, tutored, and advised students enrolled in Operations Management class

Microcomputer Laboratory Monitor, September 2004 to June 2006
Stanford University, Stanford, CA

- Guided and assisted students and faculty in the productive use of analytical, graphics, and word-processing PC software
- Served more than 100 users during peak laboratory usage

COMPUTER BACKGROUND

Proficient in use of the following PC programs, operating systems, and languages:
Windows 98 XP, RBase for DOS, Statgraphics, C+ Lotus Notes, Quattro Pro,
MS Office Suite, Harvard Graphics, MS-DOS, Netware, Pascal, BASIC, FORTRAN

page 1 of 2

AWARDS & HONORS

- Awarded $5,000 fellowship in 2004 by Education Trust
- Member of Beta Gamma Sigma (national honor society for business students)

REFERENCES

Supplied on request

Kenneth H. Crothers

80 Cavendish Drive   Madison, WI 53714   (608) 555-6034   k.crothers@xxx.com

Education

Bachelor of Arts in Architecture, December 2006
University of Wisconsin, Madison, WI

Experience

Landscape Architect, April 2006 – Present
Nancy's Nurseries and Garden Center, Madison, WI
Conduct cost estimates, develop designs for residential/commercial landscapes, and lead final design presentation for client.

Partner/Designer, January 2006 – April 2006
Self-employed home renovator, Milwaukee, WI
Developed ideas for home interior renovations and implemented ideas and designs according to local building codes.

Assistant Layout Supervisor, May 2005 – September 2005
Bradford Malls, Milwaukee, WI
Assisted in the planning and layout operation for new and existing mall and restaurant parking areas.

Site Surveyor, May 2004 – August 2004
K&R Installations, Milwaukee, WI
Installed recreational decks.

Military

United States Marine Corps, September 1994 – April 2004
Anti-armor team leader and explosives expert.

Related Skills

Operate CAD system; read wide variety of design prints.

References

Available upon request.

WILLIAM LYON COOPER

4142 Telegraph Avenue, #9
Berkeley, CA 94709
Bill.Cooper@xxx.com
(408) 555-7756

Work History

Project Manager, 2004 – Present   Environmental Systems Group, Oakland, CA

Prepare environmental assessments, facilities plans, and specialized reports.
Collect data through research and field surveys.
Conceptual design of wastewater treatment systems.

2002 – 2004   Oregon State University Bookstore, Corvallis, OR

- Began as cashier, advanced to special-order clerk; further advancement to assistant branch manager.
- Ordered stock and inventory supplies; cleared and balanced daily sales; supervised hourly employees and customer relations.
- Worked 40 hours a week while attending college for three years.

Education

December 2003

Bachelor of Science in Public Affairs, majors in Environmental Science and Environmental Affairs, Oregon State University, Corvallis, OR

- Concentration grade point average of 2.9. Courses included Biology, Chemistry, Energy and the Environment, Environmental Techniques, Geology, Hydrogeology, Lake and Watershed Management, Law and Public Policy, Physics, and Urban Development.

References

Available on request.

Lakeisha G. Prescott

58 Mahwah Drive
Newark, New Jersey 07430
L.Prescott@xxx.com
(201) 555-5297

EDUCATION

Purdue University, 1987
B.S. Industrial Management (minor in Industrial Engineering), GPA: 4.6/6.0

EMPLOYMENT SUMMARY

Approximately 20 years of experience in the fields of industrial engineering and manufacturing/process engineering

EMPLOYMENT

8/98 to Present
Central Engineering, Newark, NJ
Senior Industrial Engineer

1/98 to 8/98
Newark Steel and Wire Company, Newark, NJ
Contracted Industrial Engineer

7/97 to 12/97
Chicago Engineering, Chicago, IL
Contracted Industrial Engineer

4/94 to 5/97
Northern Design, Chicago, IL
Industrial Engineer

9/87 to 4/94
Industrial Designers, South Bend, IN
Industrial Engineer

ACCOMPLISHMENTS

Developed process for assembly and fabrication departments

Conceptualized and drew layouts and tooling for assembly and fabrication

Managed Material Review Board

Established annual budget and monthly staffing for line operations

Coordinated cost reduction program

NOLAN BRIAN KERR

930 North Leland Road • Flint, Michigan 48502 • (313) 555-7623

CAREER OBJECTIVE

A position that requires technical knowledge in the areas of design, testing, and reliability of mechanical and electrical systems in order to manufacture a quality product

EDUCATION

Purdue University, West Lafayette, Indiana
Attended: August 1993 - June 1995
Bachelor and Associate degrees in Mechanical Engineering Technology

Indiana State University, Terre Haute, Indiana
Attended: August 1991 - May 1993
Education included 20 hours of electronics and 10 hours of computer programming

WORK EXPERIENCE

Michigan Lighting, Manufacturing Engineer

(M.L. is a joint American and Japanese automotive lighting company)

- Experience includes these areas: component designs, thermoset and thermoplastic molding, tooling, material evaluation, assembly line setups, adhesive development, robot feasibilities, and customer/supplier contacts
- Familiar with foreign and domestic manufacturing concepts. Received Taguchi Design of Experiments training

Mercury Lamp Division of Ford Motor Company, Project Engineer

- Five years of experience in working with automotive lighting systems
- Performed the following functions: developed tests and implemented changes from test car and laboratory data; set up inventory systems; maintained budget, timing, and payroll records on computer; designed hardware parts for lamps; coordinated prototype parts; and designed layouts for the Forward Lighting facility
- Supervised laboratory technicians, published testing manuals and reports, performed cost-savings analysis on computer, and developed systems to monitor product performance in the field

REFERENCES

Furnished upon request

Dennis P. Warden

152 Hogarth Avenue, Apt. #7D
Flushing, NY 11367
(718) 555-5401
d.warden@xxx.com

BUSINESS EXPERIENCE

April 2001–Present
Industrial Engineer, Needham Cable, Flushing, NY

- Assist with world-class manufacturing and cell technologies implementation for rapid and continual improvement.
- Designed and programmed computerized suggestion system using Microsoft Access, reducing clerical duties.
- Coordinated cost reduction program.

October 1998–September 2000
Plant Design Engineer, Coastal Cable, New Orleans, LA

- Justified and submitted cost reduction projects.
- Served as project engineer for OSHA safety project. Supervised completion of the project on time and under budget.
- Designed spreadsheet and database programs to create monthly master production schedules and material requirements for capacity analysis and JIT planning.

June 1997–August 1998
Plant Industrial Engineer, Lawrence Metals, Tampa, FL

- Established engineering standards to increase productivity.
- Reduced the number of rejected and scrap shipments by writing detailed process sheets for operator use.

EDUCATION

Columbia University, 1996
School of Engineering and Applied Science
B.S. in Mechanical Engineering

References available on request.

Curtis S. Martinez

86 El Camino Drive ■ Austin, Texas 75090 ■ Cellular: (214) 555-7690 ■ Home: (214) 555-8929

OBJECTIVE: MIS management position with upward potential.

SUMMARY: Outstanding track record:
- Management acceptance.
- Vendor negotiations.
- Systems/programming/operations.
- Plan and policy formation.

TECHNICAL: DL1/MS, DOS/VSE, IBM, 37U/43xx, CICS, OS/MVS, C++, Windows Server, Cobol, Fortran, Mark IV, Datamanager.

APPLICATIONS: Distribution, finance, manufacturing, marketing, operations.

EXPERIENCE: *1997–Present* ■ *IBM Corporation* ■ *Austin, Texas*

Multinational Manager of Business Systems (2004–present)

- Managing multinational staff on enhancement and implementation of equipment order, control, and invoicing Timss systems developed by IBM in Europe for Latin American operations.
- Evaluated and recommended acquisition.
- Prepared cost/benefit ROI.
- Created project organization requirements.

Manager of Business Systems (1999–2004)

- Directed project managers on joint applications development for major subsidiaries.
- Retained Manager/Systems Applications responsibility.
- Programmed, purchased, or transferred applications via formal development and project methodologies.
- Conducted overseas management reviews and sold improvement ideas.
- Established centralized systems development staff in major local company.

Manager of Systems Application (1997–1999)

- Established and managed systems, programming, and operations group for HQ.

References available.

SUNIL TAHJA

48 Lawrence Hall, University of California ✧ Berkeley, CA 94720
S.Tahja@xxx.com ✧ (510) 555-0568

✧ OBJECTIVE
Development of computer and communication networks

✧ EDUCATION
University of California at Berkeley, Berkeley, CA
M.S. in Electrical Engineering, December 2005
G.P.A.: 3.8/4.0

Chambal Regional College of Engineering, Kanpur, India
B.S. in Electrical Engineering, May 2004

- ✧ Senior project: simulated a PC-based protection relay and verified various algorithms for line and phase faults on power transmission lines
- ✧ One-month industrial training at Delhi Electronics Limited, Lahore, India, in the areas of data processing, communication, and electronics

✧ BACKGROUND
Design, modeling, and analysis of centralized and distributed networks; routing and flow algorithms; switching techniques; multiple access for broadcast networks; data communication hardware and software; packet-stitched and circuit-switched networks; and satellite and local area networks

Scientific Programming on VMS, UNIX, and MS-DOS in C++, Pascal, FORTRAN, Basic, and Assembly languages

✧ EXPERIENCE
Adjunct Lecturer, Department of Computer Science, University of California at Berkeley. Instructor for an undergraduate course in FORTRAN programming. (January 2005 to May 2005)

✧ ACTIVITIES
Treasurer, IEEE Student Chapter, Kanpur, India (2002–2004)

Coordinator, National Symposium on Applications of Telecommunication in the Indian context, Kanpur, India (September 2004)

References available upon request

JAMES B. WEITZMAN

980 CARPENTER ROAD   RALEIGH, NC 27602   (919) 555-3026

J.WEITZMAN@XXX.COM

Summary

Desire estimator position with room for advancement.

Salary requirements are open.

References and photo portfolio are available.

Employment History

August 2004 - Present   Baldwin Lumber Company, Estimator/Designer

♦ Prepare takeoffs of roof and floor trusses for single-family and multifamily dwellings as well as commercial and institutional structures.

♦ Work requires the ability to read and understand all types of architectural drawings and to develop working roof or floor designs that meet the architect's requirements and the owner's budget.

January 2002 - February 2004   GMA Builders, Inc., Estimator/Drafter/Computer Operator

♦ Estimated and designed custom homes.

♦ Developed an estimating method using the computer to increase efficiency and accuracy of residential estimating.

Education

December 2001   Rochester Technical Institute

Associate Degree, with Honors, Architectural Engineering Technology

May 1999   Batavia Consolidated High School

Graduated in top 20 percent of class

Coursework in drafting and woodworking

References available upon request.

CHARLES W. WHITE

45 Cedar Pines Lane ❖ Logan, Utah 84322 ❖ Charlie.White@xxx.com ❖ (801) 555-7516

OBJECTIVE

To capitalize on my experience in surveying and develop new skills in related fields.

EDUCATION

Utah State University, Logan, Utah

Bachelor of Science Degree in Earth Science, May 2004

Areas of:	Physical Geography	Meteorology	Chemistry
	Geomorphology	Structural Geology	Glacial Geology
	Mineralogy	Oceanography	Calculus
	Physics	Wave Optics	Petrology
	Paleontology	Astronomy	

WORK EXPERIENCE

January 2002–Present ❖ L. Harvey Will, Logan, Utah—Party Chief

Responsible for three-person crews. Work involves new subdivisions, construction layout, grade work, roads, boundary surveys, stakeouts, and title and deed research.

March 2001–January 2002 ❖ Price and Casper, Ogden, Utah—Party Chief

Performed surveys of residential and commercial property.

January 2000–March 2001 ❖ Robert Beck and Associates, Provo, Utah—Assistant Surveyor

Participated in field work utilizing theodolite and transit, aerial photographs, tax maps, deeds, and sophisticated field instruments.

REFERENCES

Furnished upon request

PAUL YU

3300 Westwood Dr. ◈ *Cuyahoga Falls, OH 44221* ◈ *Paul.Yu@xxx.com* ◈ *(216) 555-6929*

OBJECTIVE

To attain a position as a designer/drafter with a highly aggressive architectural engineering firm.

SKILLS

- Design and detailing of commercial mechanical, electrical, and plumbing systems.
- Architectural plans and details and site layout.

EXPERIENCE

4/04 to present   **THE INDUSTRIAL DESIGN GROUP, INC.**

- Design development of mechanical, electrical, and plumbing systems within commercial projects.
- Produce final bid documents on multiple media and AutoCad software.
- Develop construction details for architectural and engineering concepts.
- Responsible for pictorial sections used in site development and layout.

9/00 to 3/04   **TACO BELL**

- Supervised and evaluated the performance of twenty employees.
- Scheduled employees to maintain a productive operation.
- Responsible for payroll, daily and monthly accounting, and inventory control.

EDUCATION

Cleveland Institute of Applied Sciences
A.S. in Mechanical Design and Drafting Technology, 12/04
Pursuing B.S. in Mechanical Engineering Technology

REFERENCES

Available upon request.

Scott Monroe

64 Fountain Lake Road   Gary, IN 46408   (219) 555-6823
scott.monroe@xxx.com

TITLE:

Electrical Engineer/Power Demand Maintenance

EDUCATION:

B.S.E.E., 2001, Purdue University; G.P.A. of 3.5/4.0
M.S., Global Technology Management, 2005, Northwestern University; G.P.A. of
3.6/4.0

EXPERIENCE:

BETHLEHEM STEEL, Bethlehem, PA
2004 - present   AREA MANAGER—STEELMAKING RELIABILITY
- Supervise salaried and non-salaried positions.
- Developed and implemented a new power demand system and new vacuum system.

2003 - 2004   STEEL OPERATIONS MAINTENANCE ENGINEER
- Supervised combustion, electrical, and electronics engineering.
- Investigated and solved electrical and mechanical problems.

2002 - 2003   SUPERVISOR—STEELMAKING RELIABILITY
- Responsible for regular and preventive maintenance of steelmaking equipment.
- Interfaced with support group and contractors.

2001 - 2002   ASSOCIATE MANUFACTURING ENGINEER
- Investigated furnace transformer failures.
- Incorporated new technology.

ALLENTOWN STEEL, Pittsburgh, PA
2000 - 2001   ELECTRICAL ENGINEER
- Installed quality control X-ray system.
- Designed and installed an automatic conveyor system.

GOODYEAR TIRE & RUBBER COMPANY, Akron, OH
1998 - 2000   ELECTRICAL ENGINEER
- Assisted in installation of new test wheel. Installed twelve new tire presses.

References Available

EDGAR PETERS

9 De Soot Drive
Baton Rouge, Louisiana 70805
edgar.peters@xxx.com
(504) 555-1388

OBJECTIVE

An industrial engineering position with involvement in a manufacturing environment and opportunities to advance into production management.

EDUCATION

Master of Engineering	Bachelor of Science
Tulane University, 2005	Tulane University, 2003
	Major: Industrial Engineering

EXPERIENCE

2003 to present   Alexander Steel Company, Baton Rouge, Louisiana
Associate Industrial Engineer

Provide identification and implementation of computer applications for analysis and control. Activities include computer modeling and economic and statistical analysis. Originated an operating change to increase furnace hot-blast temperature. Developed diagnostic, routing, quality control, and unit scheduling expert systems.

2002 to 2003   Packaging Systems, Inc., New Orleans, Louisiana
Part-Time Supervisor

Responsible for ten people in package-sorting activities. Supervised, evaluated, and trained sorting and audit personnel.

2000 to 2002   Production Facilities, New Orleans, LA
Student Assistant

Assisted project managers in development of new production and test facilities. Developed and documented procedures for initiating component repairs.

REFERENCES

Available upon request

BRYAN PULLMAN

43 Buffalo Bill Road   Omaha, NE 68129   (402) 555-5837   B.Pullman@xxx.com

EDUCATION

University of Nebraska at Lincoln, 2001: B.S. in geology

University of Nebraska at Lincoln, 2001–present: Graduate studies in geology, forestry, and natural resources

PROFESSIONAL EXPERIENCE

Project Geologist
Buckman & Klein Engineering, Inc., April 2002–present

- Manage environmental assessments for properties undergoing acquisition, divesture, or refinancing
- Supervise and document underground storage tank removal and subsequent contaminated soil remediation
- Design soil venting systems, groundwater recovery/treatment systems, and bioremediation programs
- Responsible for proposals, drill scheduling, material purchasing, invoicing, and client development on projects

Materials Engineering Technician
Maxwell Associates, May 2001–April 2002

Engineering Assistant
Nebraska Department of Natural Resources Division of Water,
February 2001–April 2001

ACHIEVEMENTS

- Nebraska Academy of Science: Presented and published *The Formation of the Platte Sinkhole and the Drainage Effects on Platte and Stapleton Hollows*
- Geological Society of America: Presented research project on soil development at 2001 convention

REFERENCES

Available upon request

Lionel Dean

4536 N. Wolcott St.   Chicago, IL 60640   L.Dean@xxx.com   (312) 555-7862

CAREER OBJECTIVE

A mechanical engineering position in a manufacturing/design environment.

EDUCATION

B.S., Mechanical Engineering Technology
University of Illinois at Urbana/Champaign
Major G.P.A 4.8/5.0, December 2001

EXPERIENCE

2005 - Present UNITED STATES STEEL, East Chicago, IN

HYDRAULIC/MAINTENANCE ENGINEER
Hydraulic engineer assigned as mechanical coordinator for revamp projects and development of a hydraulic training program for mechanical maintenance personnel.

Maintenance Engineer responsible for the design, procurement, and construction of various mechanical/structural projects.

Duties include development and estimate of work, selection of an engineering contractor, scheduling and cost control, development of contractor bid packages, selection of a field contractor, and overall approval and supervision of field work.

MAINTENANCE TURN SUPERVISOR
Responsibilities included supervision of bargaining unit employees who maintained a flat-roll steel finishing facility.

2001 - 2005 UNIVERSITY GROUP, Urbana, IL

MAINTENANCE SUPERVISOR
Responsibilities included repair and operation of HVAC, building utilities, grounds, and their respective equipment.

AFFILIATIONS

Member of United Steelworkers Union #322
Member, Building Trades Guild

Mark Chang

587 Cascade Drive
Portland, Oregon 97239
Mark.Chang@xxx.com
(503) 555-3578

OBJECTIVE

To obtain a position as an engineer where I can apply my knowledge of digital circuit design, programmable controllers, and microprocessors.

EMPLOYMENT

Chrysler Data Systems   Portland, Oregon

Systems Engineer. Initially worked with Electrical/HVAC group resolving computer problems, keeping inventory, and establishing the goals of the group. Now work as part of the Plant Systems group resolving problems, analyzing change requests, and writing troubleshooting documentation for an automated storage and retrieval system.

Dates: August 2004 to Present

Perkins Engineering   Eugene, Oregon

Die Detailer. Responsibilities included drawing dimensional die details, making engineering changes to die drawings and details, and running blueprints.

Dates: May 2003 to July 2004

EDUCATION

Portland State University, Portland, Oregon

Bachelor of Science degree in Electrical Engineering, May 2003

Passed the Professional Engineering Exam, April 2003

AFFILIATIONS

Institute of Electrical and Electronic Engineers

REFERENCES

Available upon request

WILLIAM J. SHAW

1810 Cedar Crest Blvd.

Lacy, WA 98503

Bill.Shaw@xxx.com

(360) 555-1479

CAREER SUMMARY

More than twenty years' experience in manufacturing, production, and assembly of medium- and high-volume stamping and fabrication operations. Supervised activities in fabrication, stamping, welding, and finishing of automotive and agricultural equipment as well as appliances. Responsible for training, scheduling, safety, work quality, material movement, and discipline.

TECHNICAL QUALIFICATIONS

Experienced with JIT, MRP, statistical process control, and automated visual inventory/scheduling concepts. Proficient in high-speed light stampings, transfer press operations, heavy stamped assemblies, welding, and testing instrumentation/procedures.

EMPLOYMENT HISTORY

Whirlpool Corporation, Seattle, WA   *8/00 to present*

    Operations/Finishing Manager

Ford Motor Company, San Leandro, CA   *6/87 to 8/00*

    Positions held: Supervisor of Cab Fabrication/Finishing, Maintenance Supervisor, and Finished Vehicle Assembly Supervisor

EDUCATION

    B.S. in Business Administration, Carnegie Mellon University, 1986

References available on request

ANA FONG

1260 PALMETTO DRIVE
ORLANDO, FL 32816
Ana.Fong@xxx.com
(305) 555-1318

OBJECTIVE

To utilize my management, marketing, and computer service experiences to make an immediate contribution as a member of a professional management team

TECHNICAL EXPERTISE

Systems: Timss, ACCESS
Hardware: IBM 309X-308X, IBM 4331, StorageTek 4400 ACS

EMPLOYMENT SUMMARY

Corporate Operations Manager
Reynolds Corporation, Orlando, FL
2002–Present

- Directed implementation of new data center and hired and trained operations and network personnel

- Coordinated hardware acquisitions and lease negotiations for all nationwide corporate facilities

- Reduced printing costs by managing a project team through the analysis, design, development, and implementation of new printing systems and design procedures

Operations Manager
Dade County Information Services Agency, Miami, FL
1999–2002

- Initiated automated problem resolution system, resulting in reduction of problems and elimination of manual systems

- Developed position titles and pay scales that resulted in identifiable career paths for operations personnel

EDUCATION

University of Miami   B.S. in Computer Science, 1998

AFFILIATIONS

- Florida Telecommunications User Association
- Association for Computer Operations Managers
- Reynolds Corporate Mentor for Partners in Education Program

REFERENCES

Available on request

PETER DAWSON

420 Calumet Avenue
Gary, IN 46408
(219) 555-6457
dawson@xxx.com

OBJECTIVE

Position in process metallurgy/quality control.

CAREER SUMMARY

Fifteen years of service with a major manufacturer of flat-rolled and tubular products in various functional areas. Highly developed skills in work organization, metallurgical process control and applications, and expertise in finishing and management of basic manufacturing.

WORK EXPERIENCE

United States Steel Corporation, Gary, IN   **1996-present**

Hot Mill Metallurgist (1998-present)

- Responsible for all aspects of hot strip mill quality including thermal practice, customer product and processing requirements, testing, and claims.
- Established new product/grade hot-rolling standards.
- Supervised hot strip mill quality control workforce, including metallurgical turn supervisor, observers, and testing personnel.

High Carbon/Alloy Metallurgist (1996-1998)

- Responsible for quality and thermal process control for all high carbon and alloy grades/products.
- Directed and coordinated slabbing and hot-rolling of customer conversion material.
- Established and developed standard operating and testing procedures for high-tech alloy application.

United States Steel Corporation, Cleveland, OH   **1988-1996**

Shipping Supervisor (1994-1996)

Responsible for processing of various sizes, lengths, and grades of tubular products.

EDUCATION

B.S. Metallurgical Engineering, Purdue University, West Lafayette, IN, 1988

page 1 of 2

AFFILIATIONS

- American Steelworkers Association
- Professional Metallurgical Engineers Guild
- Steelworkers Union #458

References available on request.

Rachel Schwartzman

125 College Way
Princeton, NJ 08545
Email: schwartz@xxx.com
Cellular: (609) 555-7854

Objective

Mechanical engineering and/or programming position involving robotics or other electromechanical systems.

Education

Princeton University, Princeton, NJ
Major: Mechanical Engineering (GPA: 3.8/4.0)
Graduation expected in May 2007.
Won graduate research fellowship to perform independent robotics research.

Experience

Summer 2006, Programmer, General Electric (Robotics Lab)
Developed a robotic work cell using linear motor robots to assemble washer-pumps at high production rates. Designed the gripper hardware for each task in the production cycle as well as all the fixturing for the parts being assembled.

Summer 2005, Computer Programmer, World Airways, Inc.
Set up monthly customer mailing system/inventory database in ACCESS and Timss.

Summer 2004, Robotics/Computer Programmer, Rutgers University
Programmed Robotic Lab equipment and vision system for horticulture research.

Honors

General Electric Scholarship, full tuition
Member, Tau Beta Pi
Member, Phi Beta Kappa

References

Available upon request

Maria Valtiera

11917 North Palace Park

Tucson, AZ 85710

Maria.Valtiera@xxx.com

(520) 555-6463

OBJECTIVE:

Seeking a challenging position in the areas of systems analysis, database management, and programming that will utilize my technical and interpersonal skills.

EDUCATION:

University of Texas
Austin, Texas

B.S. in Computer Technology, Computer Information Systems
Minors in Business and Industrial Operations
Graduated June 1999

WORK EXPERIENCE:

Carl James Associates, Indianapolis, Indiana
Associate (February 2002 to present)

Converted all operations for an Indiana municipality from Burroughs ISAM/COBOL/RPG to C++. Redesigned, rewrote, developed, and implemented all applications and new development.

Mayflower Van Lines, Indianapolis, Indiana
Programmer/Analyst (February 2001 to February 2002)

Designed, developed, and implemented reporting applications for operations, including financial and operational reporting. Responsible for PC hardware and software setup and support for 25 PCs.

Hardware Wholesalers, South Bend, Indiana
Programmer/Analyst Trainee (summer 2000)

Programmed COBOL with IDMS, created an online application using CICS and COBOL, and wrote documentation and created new applications using Easytrieve Plus and Keymaster.

REFERENCES AVAILABLE

ROBERT L. KRUSKIE

46 Washington Boulevard
Albuquerque, New Mexico 87131
Robert.Kruskie@xxx.com
505-293-0510

EDUCATION

B.S. in Civil Engineering, 1990

EXPERIENCE

KAISER HEAVY CONSTRUCTION

4200 Santa Fe Drive   Albuquerque, New Mexico 87134

6/99 to present

Senior Estimator in home office.

Handle all underground bids.

9/98 to 4/99

Special Projects Engineer on King Dam Project. Supervised excavation of underground powerhouse.

MONTGOMERY, INC.

46 Washington Boulevard   Albuquerque, New Mexico 87131

1/96 to 9/98

Consultant to heavy construction contractors on estimating, claim preparation, construction management, and design of ground support systems. Consultant to law firms on preparation of legal proceedings involving construction claims.

4/93 to 1/96

Subcontractor doing pipe jacking, small tunnels, bulkhead and stone revetments, structure grouting, grading, and site work.

R & G CONSTRUCTORS, INC.

8715 Highway 395   Reno, Nevada 89557

10/88 to 10/90

Project Engineer on Emigrant Gap Tunnel, South Lake Tahoe, California.

REGISTRATION

Professional Engineer in the following states:

- New Mexico
- District of Columbia
- Nevada

References available on request.

Michael G. Block

75 Eldridge Court
Cambridge, MA 02138

Home: (617) 555-4813
Work: (617) 555-6741
Email: mike.block@xxx.com

OBJECTIVE

To utilize my communication, problem-solving, and decision-making skills in a professional position that offers development and increasing levels of responsibility.

EDUCATION

Ivy Technical Institute - Associate Degree

Material Requirements Planning Seminars - Certificate

ITT Technical Institute - Certificate

EXPERIENCE

October 2005–Present   **Lincoln Engineering, Cambridge, MA**

Service Technician Assistant.   Assist service technicians in installing heating and air-conditioning units in various citywide industrial and residential applications. Provide pick-up and delivery service. Operate hydraulic forklift. Use acetylene/oxygen cutting torch and other related trade tools.

April 2000–September 2005   **Taylor Components Group, Concord, NH**

Programmer Technician.   Developed and maintained applications for various departments. Created screen formats for program access using FOCUS Report Writer language.

Trainer.   Provided end users with working understanding of computer. Taught in-house seminar on creating Bills of Material using Cullinet online software package.

Help Desk Technician.   Allocated, created, and deleted data sets for end users. Provided troubleshooting assistance. Served as liaison between Management Information Service and various departments.

Technical Writer.   Prepared and provided end users with step-by-step procedures for using computer. Prepared user manual for Bills of Materials seminar.

April 1995–February 2000   **Monzon Enterprises, Concord, NH**

Drafter.   Prepared detailed drawings of parts from layouts and sketches using standard drawing and drafting and measuring tools and instruments.

REFERENCES

Available Upon Request

Kevin G. Ackroyd

438 Beaver Drive, Apt. 67   University Park, PA 16802
(814) 555-9478   kevinackroyd@xxx.com

EMPLOYMENT GOAL

Full-time employment in a medium-size company that does earthwork and/or heavy construction.

EDUCATION

Penn State University

Bachelor of Science in Construction Engineering Management, 2007

RELATED EXPERIENCE

Engineer Intern, Williamsport Paving Co., Williamsport, PA. June to September 2006.

Responsible for upkeep of the job-costing system on all projects and time and material billings. Some estimating, job supervision, signing, and laboring.

Project Officer, 125th Engineer Battalion, PAANG, 2005 to present.

The officer in charge of a road construction project and a haul-in project. Duties include coordination of materials, equipment, and direct supervision of project.

Grade Checker/Laborer, White Construction Co., Wilkes-Barre, PA. July to September 2004.

Gained experience in grade checking, pipe-laying, chip-seal, and flagging.

Equipment Operator, Barron's Trenching, Altoona, PA. July to September 2004.

Operated a CASE 580 Backhoe and 450 dozer in excavation for farm drainage systems and private contract work.

LEADERSHIP, ACTIVITIES, HONORS & AWARDS

Member, AGC Student Chapter, Penn State

Commander, ROTC Drill Team

Platoon Leader, Heavy Equipment Platoon, National Guard

Recipient of a three-year AGC undergraduate scholarship

REFERENCES AVAILABLE

LEO CERVETTO

- 18 Cliff Road

- Portland, Oregon 97205

- (503) 555-3546

- leocervetto@xxx.com

PROFESSIONAL EXPERIENCE

Coordinator of Technical Services

Alliance Oregon, Inc. ■ *December 2006–Present*

In charge of asbestos program for more than 100 school buildings, involving review of existing asbestos management programs and extensive contact with school administrators in planning and implementation of timely and budget-sensitive management programs for environmental issues. Regularly conducted field surveillance and inspection activities at all sites. Trained school personnel on various environmental issues including procedures for dealing with asbestos, lead, and radon. Wrote company hazard communication, respiratory protection, and medical surveillance programs as well as standard operating procedures manuals for functions within the asbestos management program.

Industrial Hygienist

Environmental Consultants ■ *March 2004–October 2006*

Project manager position involving coordination of industrial hygiene and asbestos-related projects: bulk sampling, technical report writing, abatement project specification development, environmental compliance monitoring, and project design. Supervised technician pool and client services. Carried out wet chemistry procedures applicable to analysis of priority pollutants, both organic and inorganic, for solid and liquid matrices.

Laboratory Technician

Beaver Analytical Services ■ *June 2001–February 2004*

Responsible for preparation of solid and liquid samples for the analysis of tetrachlorodibenzodioxin. Duties included sample check-in, solid/liquid extraction, various clean-up procedures, and standards preparation.

Page 1 of 2

EDUCATION

Portland State University, graduated May 2001

Bachelor of Science
Biology major, chemistry minor
Training/Accreditation

OSHA compliance training

EPA-accredited building inspector
EPA-accredited asbestos management planner
Sampling and Evaluating Airborne Asbestos Dust certification

SPECIALTIES

- All aspects of asbestos management in residential and commercial buildings
- Air sample analysis by polarized light microscopy
- Indoor air quality evaluation
- Industrial hygiene sampling

REFERENCES AVAILABLE

WILBUR KENNEDY

▌ *619 Alameda Street*

▌ *Santa Barbara, CA 93107*

▌ *(805) 555-3428*

▌ *wilburkennedy@xxx.com*

SUMMARY

Eight years of nuclear operations experience in the U.S. Navy, followed by four years of management experience and two years of design experience in the electronics industry.

EXPERIENCE

2003 - present

Ace Electronics Group, Santa Barbara, CA

Engineer   **2006 - present**
▌ Have designed more than ten optical sensors and industry controls.
▌ Have designed circuit board layouts.
▌ Supervise the production and testing of prototypes.
▌ Supervise the maintenance of engineering department records and drawings.
▌ Work with customers to design solutions to their applications.

Production Manager   **2004 - 2006**
▌ Made planning, controlling, and staffing decisions.
▌ Supervised production of sensors and oscillators.
▌ Selected and implemented software and hardware for computer accounting of inventory.

Technician   **2003 - 2004**
▌ Tested, adjusted, and repaired optical sensors and crystal oscillators.

EXPERIENCE (cont.)

1998 - 2003

U.S. Navy

Nuclear-Powered Research Submarine   *1999 - 2003*
- Assigned as Interior Communications Officer and Computer Officer.
- Supervised and maintained underwater closed-circuit television equipment, digital computer equipment, and electronic navigation equipment.

Nuclear-Powered Submarine   *1998 - 1999*
- Operated and maintained electrical generating and distribution equipment.
- Performed vibration analysis of rotating equipment.

EDUCATION AND TRAINING
- B.S., Electronic Engineering Technology, University of California, Santa Barbara
- USN Nuclear Power School
- USN Nuclear Power Prototype
- USN Electrician's Mate "A" School

REFERENCES AVAILABLE

JUDITH W. SWENSEN

4422 Kennet Avenue ❖ Jubal, Tennessee 37232 ❖ (615) 555-4876

judithswensen@xxx.com

❖ Summary of Qualifications

Experience in providing comprehensive environmental assistance to mining operations and exploration projects. Detailed knowledge of federal environmental regulations, helping to assess compliance of subsidiary companies. Ability to conduct detailed environmental audits at mining and terminal locations.

❖ Accomplishments

Solid Waste Disposal

As disposal methods analyst, charged with determining best disposal method at each subsidiary mine. Methods chosen are site-specific and depend on depth to groundwater, percentage and types of heavy metals present in the coal ash, and column leachate test results.

Investigated and designed economical solid and hazardous waste disposal options for subsidiary companies.

Mine Drainage Treatment

Assisted subsidiaries with effective economical methods of controlling acid mine drainage from coal refuse piles and ensuring reclamation success. Conducted research with Tennessee State University to determine methods of refuse pretreatment to eliminate future AMD and have successfully installed two systems.

❖ Employment History

Senior Development Specialist, 2005 to present
Smoky Mountain Mining Company, Memphis, TN

Graduate Assistant/Lab Technician, 2003 to 2005
University of Tennessee, Chemical Engineering Department

❖ Education

University of Tennessee
Ph.D. in Chemical Engineering, 2005
B.S. in Chemistry and Physics, 2002

❖ Affiliations

Scientific Society of America
Women in Environmental Engineering
Professional Engineering Association

References provided on request

✐ Samantha T. Smith

15 E. Green Street, #333 ■ Richmond, VA 18978 ■ (804) 555-3903

samanthasmith@xxx.com

Experienced technical writer capable of producing quality

✓ Product proposals

✓ Advertising and catalog copy

✓ Technical manuals

✓ Scientific research proposals

✓ Documentation for software systems

✓ Environmental impact statements

Clients

✓ Jenkins Manufacturing, Richmond, VA

✓ Cooper Technical Publications, Atlanta, GA

✓ Electronic Design, Inc., Richmond, VA

✓ Jones & Wright Environmental, Inc., Washington, D.C.

✓ Software Solutions, Inc., Atlanta, GA

Credentials

B.A. in English, University of Wisconsin

June 2003

Minor: Computer Science

Member, Society for Technical Communications

 References and writing samples available

STANLEY TRUMBULL

3 South Sioux Trail ■ Ottawa, Ontario, Canada K1P 5N2 ■ (613) 555-1782

OBJECTIVE: A career in the field of anthropology

EDUCATION: *UNIVERSITY OF OTTAWA, Ontario, Canada*
B.A. in Anthropology expected June 2008

HONORS: Dean's List, 2006
Phillips Anthropology Award, 2006

EMPLOYMENT: *OTTAWA UNIVERSITY, Ontario, Canada*

Department of Animal Behavior

Research Assistant, 9/05–Present

Input data for animal behavior studies

Maintain lab equipment

Monitor animals and record data

OTTAWA UNIVERSITY, Ontario, Canada

Admissions Office

Student Assistant, 9/03–4/05

Conducted campus tours

Processed applications

Assisted in student recruitment and general public relations

PARKER & PARKER, Detroit, MI

Office Assistant, 6/02–9/02

Answered phones and general e-mails

Entered data using Excel spreadsheets

ACTIVITIES: Anthropology Club, 2002–Present

Student Government Representative, Fall 2001

REFERENCES: Available upon request

GRADY BISHOP

127 Golf Street, Apt. 8B
West Lafayette, Indiana 47906
gradybishop@xxx.com
Home: (317) 555-9876
Work: (317) 555-9854

OBJECTIVE: To find a challenging position in the aerospace industry that would
utilize my engineering skills

EDUCATION: Embry-Riddle Aeronautical University, Daytona Beach, FL
Degree: Bachelor of Science in Aerospace Engineering

EXPERIENCE: *January 2003 to Present*
Aeroflight International, Lafayette, IN
Title: Strength Engineer

Responsible for detailed stress analysis for engine components. Hand and finite
element methods are utilized to examine the structural adequacy of various
components of the fan and core thrust reversers (fixed and translating parts), the
composite inlet and accessory compartment doors, and the fixed fan duct.
Analysis includes static, thermal, and pressure loads in conformance with military
standards. Interface closely with the design group during the preliminary release
phase to accelerate and optimize drawings.

June 2001 to January 2003
Commercial Aircraft Program
Title: Value Engineer

Assigned to a training program to interface with manufacturing. Goal of the project
was to discover fabrication techniques and difficulties and to improve channels of
communication between engineers and manufacturing personnel. Concepts of
value engineering were used on selected intensive and repeating problems. The
project chosen was the air-conditioning system for mid-size commercial aircraft.
Cost savings realized through this program were considerable.

EXPERIENCE (cont.): *May 1999 to June 2001*
                                   Elite Aerospace Systems, Desert Palms, CA
                                   Title: Stress Engineer

Responsible for engineering analysis and structural substantiation on modifications for various commercial aircraft. Worked closely with FAA Designated Engineer Reps (DER) in design support work.

COMPUTER EXPERIENCE: Programs such as Composite, FORTRAN, NASTRAN, PATRAN and PIPELINE on both VAX and IBM.

REFERENCES: *Available*

SCOTT M. FRANK, M.D.

-------------------------------------- 983 Crestview Dr.
Osceola, IN 46544
(219) 555-9872
scottfrank@xxx.com

EDUCATION

Year	Degree	Institution
1992	B.S.	University of Cincinnati
1997	M.D.	University of Cincinnati, College of Medicine

POSTGRADUATE TRAINING

Year	Position	Institution
1997 - 2000	Residency	East Virginia Graduate School of Medicine, Norfolk, VA
2000 - 2002	Fellow	University of Iowa Nephrology Hospital, Troy, IA

PROFESSIONAL EXPERIENCE

Year	Position	Institution
2002 - Present	Private Practice in Nephrology, Dialysis, and Transplantation	Scott Frank, M.D. Health Services 8978 Foxworth St., Ste. 555 Osceola, IN 46244

APPOINTMENTS

Medical Director: Dialysis Transplantation
Osceola Medical Center, Osceola, IN
September 2004

Clinical Assistant Professor, Department of Internal Medicine
University of Osceola, Osceola, IN
January 2004

COMMITTEES

Pharmacy and Therapeutics, Osceola Medical Center
Member, 2001 - 2004
Chair, 2004 - Present

Institutional Review Board, Osceola Medical Center
Member, 1996 - 2004

COMMITTEES (cont.)

Capital Equipment, Osceola Medical Center
Member, 2004 - Present

CERTIFICATIONS AND LICENSURE

Certification

American Board of Internal Medicine - 3/26/04 - #555555
Nephrology, American Board of Internal Medicine - 11/11/02 - #555555

Licensure (current)

Indiana - 7/2/04 - #555555

Frederick P. Sroblewski

3456 Muscatel Avenue ❦ Tucson, Arizona 85718 ❦ (602) 555-6543 ❦ frederick.sroblewski@xxx.com

Background:

Award-winning technical educator and computer support professional with international experience. Able to make an outstanding contribution to your organization in the areas of:

❦ Management Information Systems
❦ Technical Education
❦ Technical Writing
❦ Computer Systems Support

Selected Qualifications:

Technical Trainer: Achieved outstanding recognition as an educator. Selected and supervised staff of instructors. Because of personal excellence in providing training for both foreign and domestic clients, additional training services were purchased in multiple modules of $100K plus.

Creator and Developer: Researched, created, packaged, and implemented training programs never before taught in areas of quality management, computer hardware, computer software, and concepts from ideas/needs to systems application.

Technical Writer: Wrote program manuals, self-taught programs, and on-the-job training manuals. Served as resource to writing staffs to evaluate and rewrite material for practical instruction.

Computer Support Specialist: Worked with computer hardware, especially in the areas of troubleshooting and repair of equipment. Maintained integrated systems from mainframe to micro, including peripherals, used throughout the industry.

Selected Career Achievements:

Training Specialist
John Zink Company (2004 - present)

❦ Create, develop, and conduct training for both employees and customers in formal and informal settings.

Page 1 of 2

Selected Career Achievements *(cont.)*:

- Evaluate courses to determine quality of content and format, as well as select appropriate staff trainers.

- Instruct clients in ten countries as well as in the United States.

Technical Trainer
U.S. Army (2000 - 2004)

- Responsible for training theory and application of electronics to nontechnical personnel, resulting in exceptional number of participants being assigned to technical responsibilities.
- Responsible for providing total systems support under all conditions for assigned duty, with a battlefield support system.

Education:

U.S. Army Electronic Training, 2001 - 2004
Achieved highest score of any student during school's 15-year history.

Special Training and Expertise:

- Special-purpose computers
- Supercomputer integrated systems
- Mainframes through micros
- Peripheral equipment
- Personal computer applications

References:

Furnished upon request.

Greg Gold

1661 Green Street
Cedar Rapids, IA 53309
(319) 555-2909 (Home)
(319) 555-8888 (Work)
greggold@xxx.com

JOB OBJECTIVE: Engineering Technician/Camera Operator

OVERVIEW: Experience with all camera operations for film and video. Skills include studio lighting, set design, film editing, dubbing, gaffing, audio-video switching, mixing, and technical troubleshooting. Creative non-linear editor using Broadware, Avid, and Lightworks. Also familiar with still image digital correction tools, including Photoshop.

EXPERIENCE: *WCED-TV, Cedar Rapids, IA*
Engineering Assistant, July 2005–present

Drawbridge Productions, Des Moines, IA
Assistant Camera Operator, June–July 2003

WWOR Radio, Jackson, MS
Engineer, September 2001–June 2002

EDUCATION: Jackson University, Jackson, MS
B.A. in Communication Arts, June 2005

REFERENCES: Available on request

Ernest Martin

4366 South Street

Detroit, MI 48062

(313) 555-9698

ernestmartin@xxx.com

Career Goal: To obtain a position teaching dental hygiene

Education: Temple University, Philadelphia, PA
M.S. Dental Hygiene, 2004

Western Michigan University, Kalamazoo, MI
B.S. Dental Hygiene, June 2002

Experience: *June 2004 - Present*
Western Michigan University, Kalamazoo, MI
Instructor of Dental Hygiene Classes: oral anatomy,
periodontology, and physiology

September 2002 - May 2004
Western Michigan University, Kalamazoo, MI
Graduate Assistant
Duties: teaching section in periodontology and physiology,
grading assignments and quizzes, and recording
attendance for lecture periods

References: Available upon request

EDWARD J. PIERCE

1456 Burlington Ave. ■ *Cincinnati, OH 45642* ■ *(513) 555-8976* ■ *edwardpierce@xxx.com*

CAREER OBJECTIVE

To utilize my management, marketing, and computer service experience to make an immediate contribution as a member of a professional management team.

OPERATING SYSTEMS EXPERTISE

MVS (OS/390, z/OS), Unix, VM, VSE, WebSphere (MQSeries, WAS), VTAM, TCP/IP, CICS, database internals (DB2, IMS, etc.)

ADDITIONAL SKILLS

Unix Systems Administrator, Solaris, AIX, Veritas, NetBackup, IBM pSeries servers, IBM, IBM pSeries

CAREER SUMMARY

Operations Manager: 2004–Present
Genair Corporation, Cincinnati, OH

Achievements:

■ Directed implementation of new data center and hired and trained operations and network personnel. Brought online ten months ahead of schedule.
■ Reduced printing costs by 50 percent, resulting in an annual savings of $1.5 million, by managing a project team through the analysis, design, development, and implementation of new printing systems and procedures.
■ Installed corporate telecommunication systems, including PBXs, key systems, and national contract with a major carrier, resulting in a savings of over $1 million.
■ Planned and monitored annual operating budget, supervising technical staff consisting of 25 supervisors, analysts, operators, and remote schedulers.

1 of 2

CAREER SUMMARY (cont.)

Operations Manager: 1995–2004
Information Services Agency, Dayton, OH

Achievements:

■ Initiated automated problem resolution system, resulting in reduction of recurring problems and elimination of tedious manual system.
■ Developed position titles and pay scales that resulted in identifiable career paths for operations personnel.

EDUCATION

Computer Science Degree from Rose-Hulman Institute of Technology, Terre Haute, Indiana

Master in Business from University of Notre Dame, South Bend, Indiana

PROFESSIONAL COURSES

Managing Data Processing (IBM)

Data Processing Operations Management (IBM)

Turning Telephone Costs into Profits (University of Notre Dame)

PROFESSIONAL AFFILIATIONS

ITUA: Indiana Telecommunications User Association

AFCOM: Association for Computer Operations Managers

REFERENCES AVAILABLE UPON REQUEST

EDUARDO LOPEZ

6 E. Columbus Dr.

College Park, MD 20740

(410) 555-3938

eduardolopez@xxx.com

Goal: *Research technician position that allows me to use*
                     my training in physics

Education: University of Maryland, College Park, MD

                     B.S., Physics, June 2006

                     Relevant Coursework

                     ❖ Plasma Physics
                     ❖ Medical Instrumentation
                     ❖ Statistics
                     ❖ Research Methodology

Honors: Dean's List

                     Sigma Pi Sigma, Physics Honor Society

Experience: University of Maryland, Physics Department

                     Research Associate ❖ June 2006 to present

                     Conduct literature research and create literature studies to
                     support work of department. Record and analyze research data.
                     Contribute to technical reports and publications.

                     Huntington Burroughs Pharmaceutical, Inc.

                     Student Intern ❖ Summer 2004

                     Assisted senior researcher with data input, statistical analysis,
                     and computer model development.

References: Available on Request

EARLE F. ABLE

6255 N. Paulina St. ■ Chicago, IL 60636

Home: (312) 555-4948 ■ Cellular: (312) 555-4897

Email: earleable@xxx.com

OBJECTIVE

To attain a position as a designer and drafter with a highly aggressive, goal-oriented architectural engineering firm

SKILLS

Design and detailing of commercial, mechanical, electrical, and plumbing systems
Architectural plan and details and site layout

CAREER EXPERIENCE

May 2003 to Present   Engineering Development Design

Position: Designer Drafter

Duties: Design development of mechanical, electrical, and plumbing systems within commercial projects. Produce final bid documents on multiple medias and AutoCAD 2004 and Cabinet Vision software. Develop construction details for architectural and engineering concepts. Also responsible for pictorial sections used in development and layout.

EDUCATION

B.S. Mechanical Engineering Technology
University of Illinois–Champaign, 2003

A.S. Mechanical Design and Drafting Technology
Indianapolis Community College, 2001

REFERENCES FURNISHED UPON REQUEST

LAMAR FISHER ★ lamarfisher@xxx.com

Campus Address ★ 8223 Green Street ★ Pasadena, CA 91125 ★ (818) 555-7879
Home Address ★ 93 West Fourth Street ★ Long Beach, CA 90808 ★ (213) 555-9876

EDUCATION

B.S. in Civil Engineering, June 2005
California Institute of Technology, Pasadena, CA
G.P.A. 3.67

WORK EXPERIENCE

August 2005-Present
Project Engineer, Welding Corp., Culver City, IA

Main projects consisted of bridge re-decking and finalizing the construction of a cut-and-cover tunnel. Responsibilities included:

★ Coordination of all subcontractors and suppliers with JBC and DOT
★ Scheduling weekly quantity surveys
★ Estimating weekly budget reports
★ Interpretation of drawings and specifications

January 2000-August 2005
Assistant Project Manager, Grote Construction, Duluth, MN
Responsibilities included:

★ Estimating costs
★ Quantity take-off
★ Crew sizing
★ Scheduling
★ Job cost control subcontracting
★ Quantity surveys
★ Design and determination of construction methods

HONORS AND AFFILIATIONS

★ Chi Epsilon (XE) National Civil Engineering Honor Society
★ Dean's Honor List, College of Engineering
★ American Society of Civil Engineers (ASCE)

COMPUTER SKILLS

Proficient with Macintosh and IBM computers, associated software programs. PASCAL, C++, FORTRAN programming

REFERENCES AVAILABLE ON REQUEST

ELIZABETH ENGLE

2316 King Street
Richardson, TX 75080
(972) 555-2552
elizabethengle@xxx.com

GOAL

Petroleum engineering position with small, independent oil exploration and production company

EDUCATION

University of Texas at Dallas
B.S. in Petroleum Engineering, expected May 2007

Coursework:
Petroleum Engineering Design
Rocks and Fluids
Reservoir Modeling
Reservoir Engineering
Secondary Recovery
Drilling Design and Production

ADDITIONAL SKILLS

- Ability to interpret surveillance results and identify intervention opportunities
- Experience performing rig and non-rig (coil tubing) workovers, including gas and water shut-offs, plugs, straddle liners, tubing patches/repair, pulling and running new tubing

WORK EXPERIENCE

University of Texas at Dallas
Physics Department Lab Assistant, 2002–2005
Assisted professors in the Physics Department with lab experiments and general office work

MEMBERSHIPS

- Society of Petroleum Engineers
- Engineering Club

REFERENCES AVAILABLE

Evelyn Moore

• •

4366 South Street • Detroit, Michigan 48062 • (313) 555-9698

• Career Goal •

To obtain a position as a secondary-school instructor in the areas of
Science and Computer Science

• Education •

September 2004 to present
Western Michigan University, Kalamazoo, Michigan
Secondary Education Curriculum
Biology Major, Computer Science Minor

September 2000 to June 2004
Littlefield Public School, Albert, Michigan
Graduated salutatorian, June 2004

• Work Experience •

February 1999 to present
McDonald's, Kalamazoo, Michigan

Swing Manager. Duties: cash audits, deposits, quality control of product, customer
relations, supervision of employees, inventory and ordering of supplies, maintenance of
restaurant appearance, register operations, and associated paperwork

May 2000 to Present
Computer Science Department, Western Michigan University, Kalamazoo, Michigan

Computer Operator. Duties: software inventory and evaluation, programming, entering
and updating files, journal photocopying, and article synopsis

• References •

Available upon request

EDWARD DUMPHY

566 Perry Boulevard   Altus, Oklahoma 74170
(918) 555-7809   Fax (918) 555-7778   edwarddumphy@xxx.com

OBJECTIVE

To manage heavy highway construction projects as a field engineer.

EDUCATION

Purdue University, Bachelor of Science, Construction Management, 6/03

Related Coursework

Temporary Structures	Electrical/Mechanical Systems
Construction Equipment	Heavy Construction Estimating
Soils in Construction	Legal Aspects in Construction

EXPERIENCE

Willibros Butler Engineers, Inc., Altus, Oklahoma
Project Engineer, 6/04 to present

Interstate 465 Widening Project; contract value $55 million. Responsible for internal and subcontractor payletter quality, subcontractor negotiations with the State of Oklahoma Department of Transportation, and subcontractor scheduling. Produced weekly and monthly cost/quantity reports. Processed extra work bills and time cards. Managed punch list and construction crews. Assisted project superintendent in selling of job.

Rock Ware Construction Company, Oklahoma City, Oklahoma
Assistant Operations Manager, 5/02 to 6/04

Responsible for residential demolition, installation of concrete footings, drywall, and painting. Performed concrete quantity takeoffs and job setup/preplanning. Practical understanding of construction problems. Developed teamwork skills.

Windsor Shipping Company, Windsor, Ontario, Canada
Shipping and Receiving Coordinator, Summers 2000 and 2001

Responsible for all phases of shipping and receiving. Packaged merchandise and performed computerized inventory control. Processed purchase orders. Served as forklift operator and truck driver and in various clerical capacities. Developed understanding of contractual relationships.

REFERENCES AVAILABLE UPON REQUEST

David T. Sanchez

10001 W. Edina Ave.
Edina, MN 53989
(612) 555-5453
davidsanchez@xxx.com

STRENGTHS

Excellent communication and people skills

Strong photographic and processing skills

Academic and hands-on training in commercial art

Computer literate, with working knowledge of QuarkXPress,
Adobe Photoshop, Dreamweaver, and all Microsoft Office products

EDUCATION

University of Minnesota, St. Paul, MN

B.A. in Commercial Art, conferred May 2007

WORK EXPERIENCE

Minneapolis magazine, Minneapolis, MN
Commercial Artist, Summers 2004–present

University of Minnesota, St. Paul, MN
Designer, University Publications, 2003

University of Minnesota, St. Paul, MN
Photographer, Student Gazette, 2002–2003

WORKSHOPS

Website Design Seminar, University of Minnesota, 2006

Illustration Workshop, Art Institute of Chicago, 2004

Midwest Design Seminar, Northern Illinois University, 2004

REFERENCES AVAILABLE

TOM NGUYEN

543 Hillside Drive
Palo Alto, CA 94304
(415) 555-9876
tomnguyen@xxx.com

OBJECTIVE

To apply rigorous quantitative methods and models to strategic planning issues

EDUCATION

Columbia School of Engineering and Applied Science
B.S. in Operations Research
Concentration: Computer Science
Degree Expected: June 2007

Courses Taken:

- Mathematical Programming
- Data Structures and Algorithms
- Accounting and Finance
- Production-Inventory Planning and Control

COMPUTER SKILLS

Languages: BASIC, C++, FORTRAN, PASCAL

Hardware: DEC-29, Sun Work Station, IBM, and Macintosh

Software: Microsoft Office, Access, Timss

Operating System: MS Windows 98 through Windows XP, UNIX, DOS

EXPERIENCE

Research Assistant to Professor Samuel Silvers
Department of Operations Research
Columbia University, New York, NY

- Developed and implemented performance analysis of scheduling
- Designed scheduling system for university laboratories

REFERENCES

Available upon request

DAN LUI

17 Dinge Road   Terre Haute, IN 52211

317/555-1331 (Home)   317/555-2339 (Office)   danlui@xxx.com

OBJECTIVE

A position in the field of electrical engineering with an emphasis on aviation electronic systems

EDUCATION

B.S. in Electrical Engineering, May 2005
Rose-Hulman Institute of Technology, Terre Haute, IN
G.P.A. 3.75
Graduated with Honors

WORK EXPERIENCE

C & S Industrial Design Consultants, Richardson, TX
Summer Intern, 2004
Assisted in research and development department of aviation electronics firm. Input data, typed performance specifications reports, calibrated lasers, and maintained test equipment.

Rose-Hulman Institute of Technology, Terre Haute, IN
Assistant to the Director of Financial Aid, 2002 – 2004
Processed applications. Handled general office duties.

ACTIVITIES

President of Student Chapter of Institute of Electrical and Electronics Engineers

Peer Advisor, Engineering Department

REFERENCES

Available upon request

Darnell Grant

800 York Ave. South ◆ Minneapolis, MN 55410 ◆ (612) 555-7908 ◆ darnellgrant@xxx.com

◆ *Education*

B.S. Mechanical Engineering Technology, University of Minnesota, 2002
GPA: 5.75/6.00

◆ *Employment*

6/02 to present: Technastar Design Development

Development and Design Engineer (7/03 to present)

Responsible for the design and applications of product components for automotive plastic body panels. This includes recommending design changes and testing product for reliability and durability.

Project Engineer (6/02 to 7/03)

As a project engineer I was involved in manufacturing procedures, processing improvements, and troubleshooting production problems for tooling. I managed maintenance activities and vendor contracts for production tooling.

◆ *Technical Skills*

Computer—2D and 3D AutoCAD, BASIC, C++, MS Office Suite, VPN

◆ *Affiliations*

Member of Society of Automotive Engineers
Member of Society of Plastics Engineers

References available on request

ADAM CANTOR ✦ *adamcantor@xxx.com*

Work Address:

Department of Chemistry
University of Vermont
Burlington, VT 16901

OBJECTIVE

To obtain a position as a senior research and development chemist in the fields of polymer or physical chemistry.

EDUCATION

Ph.D., University of Vermont, 2005   Physical Chemistry, Dynamic Light Scattering Study of Ternary Polymer Solutions

B.S. in Chemistry, Middlebury College, 2002   Minors: Mathematics, Physics

EXPERIENCE

Research Assistant, June 2002 to August 2005
University of Vermont, Department of Chemistry

✦ Studied semi-dilute poly (n-alkyl isocyanate) solutions containing a linear polystyrene probe polymer.
✦ Examined concentration, molecular weight, and temperature dependences of the ternary solutions. Performed dynamic and static light scattering measurements.
✦ Characterized solutions using FTIR, UV, viscometry, and differential refractometry.
✦ Assisted in design, assembly, and maintenance of experimental instruments.
✦ Administered laboratory computer systems (UNIX, VMS, Macintosh, MS/DOS).

EXPERIENCE (cont.)

Health and Safety Representative, June 2001 to January 2002
University of Vermont, Department of Chemistry

+ Implemented laboratory safety measures, prepared chemical inventories, and provided personal safety instruction.
+ Aided in development of departmental safety film.

Teaching Assistant for Physical Chemistry, Laboratory,
June 2001 to December 2002
Middlebury College, Department of Chemistry

Head TA and Course TA: First-Year Chemistry, Organic Chemistry

HONORS

+ Member, Beta Kappa Nu Fraternity
+ Recipient, Chemical Engineering Scholarship of America
+ National Merit Scholar

REFERENCES

Furnished on Request

Alicia Curtiss

9867 High Drive 🖉 Lexington, Kentucky 40506

(415) 555-8712 🖉 aliciacurtiss@xxx.com

OBJECTIVE:

A position in research and development with a company interested in wide applications of polymeric materials. Possibility for move into management preferred.

EDUCATION:

University of Kentucky, Lexington, Kentucky   M.S., Chemical Engineering, 2006

Louisiana Tech University, Ruston, Louisiana   B.S., Chemical Engineering, 2004

EXPERIENCE:

July 2006–present

University of Kentucky, Department of Chemical Engineering, Lexington, Kentucky

Research Assistant, laboratory of Dr. R. Pierce

🖉 Study structures formed by diblock copolymers in a solvent selective for one block.

🖉 Use light, x-ray, and neutron scattering to determine micelle structure as a function of solution conditions.

🖉 Compare the spherical micelles to structures predicted for multi-armed star polymers.

May 2004–September 2006

University of Kentucky, Department of Chemical Engineering, Lexington, Kentucky

Research Assistant

🖉 Studied properties of monolayer and multilayer films of alkanoic acids and alkylsiloxanes on solid surfaces.

References on request

Allen Day

88 State Street
Carmel, Indiana 46032
(317) 555-3175
allenday@xxx.com

OBJECTIVE

To obtain a position in information systems, software design/development, or a related area utilizing my computer programming language skills.

EDUCATION

Allegheny College, Meadville, Pennsylvania
B.S., Computer Science
Graduation Date: June 2006

EXPERIENCE

Summer 2004

City of Reading, Reading, Pennsylvania. Management Information Systems Intern.

Duties included personal computer assembly and setup (hardware and software installation) as well as system troubleshooting. Involved significant user interaction and operating system knowledge. Worked on IBM PC ATOs and XTOs, HP Bectra PCOs using MS-DOS 3.3.

Summer 2003

Indiana University, Indianapolis, Indiana. Student Programmer.

Developed application that aids in vision/perception research by performing linear transformations to bitmap images. Consultant to supervisor.

Summer 2002

Indiana University, Indianapolis, Indiana. Research Programmer.

Developed an IBM application for desktop security and screen-saver.

SKILLS SUMMARY

Computers: C++, Pascal, Lisp. Also familiar with DOS, Linux/Unix, Active Directory, and network devices. Procedural, Functional object-oriented programming. LightSpeed, MDS environments.

REFERENCES

Available on Request

JEFFREY KALLEN

88 Waverly Road
Huntington, IN 46872
(317) 555-9876
jkallen@xxx.com

OBJECTIVE

A position in the architectural/engineering/interiors field with emphasis in the CADD environment.

EXPERIENCE

4/05 - Present: Tad Technical Services (Dow Chemical Company) as a CADD drafter.
Working on a team, my duties are revising drawings to "as built" status. Working with Digital 3100 computer running Autotrol Release 8.2 software on VAXNMS V5.3-1 operating system. Experience with Intergraph Microstation.

1/05 - 4/05: Manpower Technical Services (DBA Architects, Inc.) as a CADD drafter.

Duties included drafting up revisions on floor plans, reflected ceiling plans, schedules, and details on various projects. Worked with a Compaq computer running Autocad software.

7/04 - 1/05: SAL, Inc., as a CADD drafter.

Duties included space planning, details, and product design of various fast-food restaurants. Worked with a Compaq computer running Cadmaza software. Some exposure to Unix on Sun Sparcstation.

9/03 - 6/04: Boeing Products, Inc., as a CADD drafter (Autocad).

10/02 - 8/03: West's Architects, Inc., as a CADD drafter (Autocad).

EDUCATION

Syracuse University, NY
M.S., Operations Research

Stanford University, Stanford, CA
M.Sc., Statistics

Duke University, NC
B.Sc., Mathematics

Page 1 of 2

SKILLS

Knowledge of C++, SQL Server, Basic, COBOL. Working knowledge of FORTRAN, Pascal, Excel, Lotus Notes

MEMBERSHIPS

Operations Research Society of America

Society for Industrial and Applied Mathematics

American Association of Computer Professionals

REFERENCES

A detailed list of professional references will be provided on request.

Alexander Ho

986 Parker Lane ❖ Work (415) 555-2939

Walnut Creek, CA 94595 ❖ Home (415) 555-9875 ❖ alexanderho@xxx.com

---

❖ s u m m a r y

Intimate knowledge of microcomputer industry and applications software. More than ten years of broad international business experience with Fortune 500 corporations. Also fluent in Mandarin Chinese, good command of Japanese and Thai.

Successful accomplishments in:
- ❖ Feasibility Studies
- ❖ Office Automation
- ❖ Multinational Manufacturing
- ❖ Economic Recovery and Product Positioning and Pricing
- ❖ Analysis and Control
- ❖ Strategic Planning and Competitive Analysis
- ❖ Marketing Plans and Strategies

❖ e x p e r i e n c e

❖ *Hocorp International, Inc., Walnut Creek, CA*
President, 2005 - Present
Founded consulting and marketing firm to evaluate business problems, determine software requirements, and develop microcomputer systems to meet clients' needs.

❖ *Intercorp, Inc., Los Angeles, CA*
Manager, New Product Programs, 2002 - 2005
Responsible for product evaluation, assessment of marketing potential, and development of product feasibility studies. Completed feasibility study on 9500 Electronic Printing System for the Pacific Rim area, which led to the development of a new market area. Evaluated marketing strategies for microcomputer products in open-market countries.

❖ *Manager, Field Pricing, 2000 - 2002*
Developed, evaluated, and recommended strategic and tactical pricing actions enabling affiliates to exceed targeted profits. Developed and implemented major account pricing strategy for Malaysia that resulted in an increase on major accounts and a reduction in cancellations.

❖ *Manager, Commercial Analysis, 1998 - 2000*
Direct responsibility for long-range competitive forecast for group of 25 affiliates. Measured performance of current products and competitive practices, and identified risks and opportunities to business strategies.

❖ e d u c a t i o n

M.B.A., 1998
University of Georgia, Athens, GA

B.S., 1997
Notre Dame University, South Bend, IN
Major: Industrial Administration

B.A., 1994
City College, Chicago
Major: Marketing

❖ REFERENCES AVAILABLE UPON REQUEST ❖

John J. Allen ❧ johnallen@xxx.com

Present Address ❧ 765 Fifth Street ❧ Washington, D.C. 20016-8001 ❧ (202) 555-2213
Permanent Address ❧ 28 Octavia Terrace ❧ Washington, D.C. 20019 ❧ (202) 555-9737

❧ Objective

Full-time position as a medical writer for a pharmaceutical company, medical school, textbook publisher, or government agency.

❧ Education

George Washington University
Currently pursuing M.S. in technical writing with a concentration in biology.

Whitman College
B.S. with Highest Distinction in English, May 2006

❧ Experience

Eli Lilly and Company, Indianapolis, IN ❧ Summer 2004 ❧ Summer Intern
Analyzed new product data and prepared reports for in-house use by sales staff. Interviewed researchers and prepared articles for company publications.

Washington Post, *Washington, D.C. ❧ Summer 2003 ❧ Summer Intern*
Wrote columns on health fads, fitness, and new drugs.

❧ Credentials

❧ American Medical Writers Association certificates in pharmaceutical writing and editing

❧ Member, American Medical Writers Association

❧ Editor, Whitman College newspaper

References and Writing Samples on Request

Charles Andawa

4783 West Maple   *Baltimore, MD 21218*   *(410) 555-2983*

Objective

A position in chemical engineering with an environmental engineering organization.

Recent Experience

2005–Present   *Senior Project Manager, PPD, Inc., Baltimore, MD*

- Report to senior vice president of engineering.
- Supervise 32 employees.
- Direct, supervise, administer, and manage projects from inception to startup, including new chemical process equipment manufacturing.
- Assist sales department in reviewing the system process design, scheduling, engineering, and costs before final proposal is presented to client.
- Conceive, initiate, and develop chemical formations for nontoxic solutions for use in oil recovery and recycling.
- Formulated empirical equations and design criteria for the system, which resulted in a sevenfold increase in company sales over the last five years.
- Train project engineers and project managers to design and manage projects.

2002–2005   *Senior Project Engineer, Moreland Chemical, Annapolis, MD*

- Project experience included pulp liquor evaporation system operations, sand reclamation systems, waste wood utilization to manufacture charcoal, sewage sludge oxidation, waste oxidation, and heat recovery.
- Responsible for planning, scheduling, process design, and specifications.

Education

1999, B.S., M.S., Chemical Engineering Michigan Technical University, Houghton, MI

References

Available by request.

ALICIA ANDERSON

- 2411 White Street
- Des Plaines, IL 60016
- (847) 555-8368
- aliciaanderson@xxx.com

SUMMARY

Experienced freelance technical writer seeking new clients.

SKILLS

- Development of product proposals
- Content and copyediting of technical documents
- Revision and fact-checking of technical manuals
- Research projects
- Documentation for software products
- Creation of revision reports for technical engineers

COMPUTER SCIENCE BACKGROUND

COBOL ■ PL/1 ■ DB2 ■ BASIC ■ RPG III ■ C++
■ BAL ■ FileAid ■ Ada ■ CAD/CAM

OTHER CREDENTIALS

B.S. in Computer Science, University of Wisconsin, June 1999

Member, Society for Technical Communication

REFERENCES

Writing samples, client list, and references on request.

Jason Baxter

93 West Fourth Street
Long Beach, California 90808
(213) 555-9876
jasonbaxter@xxx.com

EDUCATION

- Bachelor of Science in Cytotechnology, June 2003
- California Institute of Technology, Pasadena, California
- GPA 3.65
- Relevant Courses: bacteriology, physiology, anatomy, histology, embryology, zoology, genetics, chemistry, and computer classes

WORK EXPERIENCE

- Cytotechnologist, June 2005 to present
- Circle Center Research Laboratory, Culver City, California
- Duties: Identifying cell specimens collected by fine-needle aspiration and report findings to the pathologist. Using computers to measure cells, a new technique that is being developed at Circle Center Research Laboratory.

CERTIFICATION

The International Academy of Cytology
National Certification Agency for Medical Laboratory Personnel

HONORS

Dean's Honor List, six semesters

REFERENCES

Available upon request

BRUCE CATT

■ 6543 Maple Street ■ Greenwood, Indiana 46142

■ Phone: (317) 555-1123 ■ brucecatt@xxx.com

EDUCATION

■ B.S. Geology, Miami University, Oxford, Ohio: 2003

■ Graduate Studies in Geology, Oberlin College, Oberlin, Ohio

■ Classes in Forestry and Natural Resources, Ohio Northern University, Ada, Ohio

■ OSHA 29 CFR 1910.120 training

PROFESSIONAL EXPERIENCE

Project Geologist
Computers & Structures, Inc., April 2003–present

■ Responsibilities include managing over 200 environmental assessments for properties undergoing acquisition or refinancing.

■ Supervise and document underground storage tank removal and closure, and subsequent contaminated soil remediation.

■ Responsible for remedial investigations including subsurface investigations to delineate the extent of soil contamination, design and installation of monitoring well systems, groundwater sampling and analysis, soil gas surveys, and geophysical studies.

■ Ability to design soil venting systems, groundwater recovery/treatment systems, and bioremediation programs.

■ Project management responsibilities include proposals, drill scheduling, material purchasing, invoicing, and client development.

AFFILIATIONS

■ Ohio Academy of Science

■ Geological Society of America

References are available and will be furnished upon request.

Maria Black •••••••••••••••••••••••••

Address:	1419 Cedar Drive
	Dayton, OH 45226
Phone:	(513) 555-8754
Email:	mariablack@xxx.com

Qualifications: Bachelor of Science in Pharmacy, 2002

School of Pharmacy: Dayton University

Special Award: Merrell Dow Dayton School of Pharmacy's Annual Award for Excellence, 2004

Previous Experience:

Hooks Pharmacy	Summer Student
Dayton, OH	10 weeks, 2004
Royal Hospital	Summer Student
Dayton, OH	8 weeks, 2002
Ohio Drug	Saturday Staff
Dayton, OH	September 1999–January 2002

Present Position: Pharmacy Graduate Intern Program
Dayton Community Hospital
Dayton, OH

Interests: My main interest is in clinical pharmacy. During my intern year, I have attended Dayton University evening classes on clinical pharmacy and an Ohio State University course in ambulance first aid.

References: Available on request.

BRADLEY Q. TRAPP

1726 Willow Springs Walk ◈ Blue Springs, MD 64015
◈ (816) 555-9997 ◈ bradleytrapp@xxx.com

OBJECTIVE

Senior Executive—Construction/Engineering

SUMMARY

Executive with diversified construction contract management achievements in a variety of industrial, refinery, petrochemical, and power generation projects. Demonstrated ability to contribute to profitable operation and growth in accordance with short- and long-term goals. A leader with innovative, analytical, and communication skills, with dynamic results in cost-sensitive critical processes and special projects.

PROFESSIONAL EXPERIENCE

Lambert Sky Supply, Inc., Blue Springs, MD
Divisional Vice President of Sales, 2003–present

◈ Complete profit and loss and operational responsibility for division of this equipment-leasing company.
◈ Created and implemented a strategic business plan for company operations throughout west central United States (20 states), resulting in the development of 50 new accounts.
◈ Increased utilization and occupancy rate of company properties from 50 percent to 95 percent during five-year period.
◈ Increased overall revenues by 25 percent between 2003 and 2005.

Reasoners, Inc., White Plains, NY
Executive Manager, 1999–2003

◈ Developed a professional project management program to utilize existing company resources and provide for diversification. The program outlined in depth a series of options for owners' use in their building programs, from conceptual through start-up phase, providing for increased project utilization and reduced building cost.

PROFESSIONAL EXPERIENCE *(continued)*

Public Service Iowa, Cedar Rapids, IA
Vice President and Director, 1996–1999

- Complete operational responsibility for this construction and engineering company.
- Supervised engineering, estimating, and construction of many multi-million-dollar industrial projects.
- Directed overall operations to effect a three-year growth by 100 percent, to a total of $50 million.
- Developed and implemented administrative and financial controls to effect significant annual savings for construction projects.

Western Systems, Tempe, AZ
Manager of Construction, 1994–1996

- Represented this construction company in a joint venture of power plant construction.
- Directed construction of six 500-megawatt power plants throughout the Midwest.
- Created and implemented cost reduction actions for plant construction that resulted in a 25 percent reduction in per-megawatt cost, as compared to the national average.

EDUCATION

B.S. Civil Engineering ❖ Michigan State University, 1990

References Available

CHRISTOPHER KNIGHT

1700 W. Armadillo St. ❧ San Diego, CA 90087 ❧ (619) 555-9000

christopherknight@xxx.com

OBJECTIVE

To obtain a position as Vice-President of Public Relations with an aeronautical corporation.

AREAS OF EXPERIENCE

Marketing Development

- ❧ Initiated and supervised sales programs for aircraft distributors selling aircraft to businesses throughout the western United States.

- ❧ Managed accounts with a profit range of $100,000 to $1,000,000, including Dow Chemical, Landston Steel, Mercury Company, Berkeley Metallurgical, and Ford Motor Company.

- ❧ Demonstrated to customer companies how to use aircraft to coordinate and consolidate expanding facilities.

- ❧ Introduced and expanded use of aircraft for musical tours.

Public Relations

- ❧ Handled all levels of sales promotion, corporate public relations, and training of industry on company use of aircraft.

- ❧ Managed promotions, including personal presentations, radio and TV broadcasts, news stories, and magazine features.

Pilot Training

- ❧ Taught primary, secondary, and instrument flight in single and multi-engine aircraft.

EMPLOYMENT HISTORY

Hughes Aircraft, Inc., San Diego, CA
Sales Manager and Chief Pilot
2003 to present

Boeing Corporation, Kansas City, MO
Assistant Manager of Promotion
2001 to 2003

1 of 2

EMPLOYMENT HISTORY *(continued)*

American Airlines, Dallas, TX
Pilot
1998 to 2001

United States Air Force, Houston, TX
Flight Instructor
1990 to 1998

PROFESSIONAL LICENSE

Airline Transport Rating 14352-60

Single, Multi-Engine Land

Flight Instructor - Instrument

EDUCATION

University of Texas, Houston, TX
B.A. in History, 1985

MILITARY SERVICE

United States Air Force
1987 to 1992

REFERENCES

Available on request

CHARLES D. STILES

■ 8765 South East Street ■

■ Ada, OH 45810 ■

■ (419) 555-9876 ■

■ charlesstiles@xxx.com ■

CAREER OBJECTIVE A position that requires technical knowledge in the areas of design, testing, and reliability of mechanical and electrical systems in order to produce a quality product.

EDUCATION Ohio Northern University, Ada, OH ■ B.S. in Mechanical Engineering Technology, 2004

Ohio Northern University ■ Have completed 21 hours of electronics and 15 hours of computer programming.

WORK EXPERIENCE Shepherd Engineering, Tulsa, OK ■ 2004 to present

Responsibilities include:
- Component designs
- Thermoset and thermoplastic molding
- Tooling evaluation
- Assembly line setups
- Adhesive development
- Robot feasibilities
- Supplier contacts

Matrix Engineering, Ada, OH ■ 2001 to 2004

Responsibilities included:
- Traveling to various engineering facilities to develop tests
- Setting up inventory systems
- Maintaining budget
- Supervising laboratory technicians
- Publishing testing manuals and reports

■ **References available upon request** ■

Lisa Bronowski

1261 W. Argyle St. ❖ Chicago, IL 60640 ❖ Home: (312) 555-4948

Cell: (312) 555-4897 ❖ Email: bronowski@xxx.com

❖ OBJECTIVE ❖

I hope to utilize my communication, problem-solving, and computer skills in an entry-level position with opportunities for advancement.

❖ EDUCATION ❖

ITT Business Institute
Associate Degree in Business, June 2005

❖ EXPERIENCE ❖

5/05 to Present, Office Assistant ❖ **Service Software, Inc.**

Assist software design specialists. General clerical duties, including answering phone and creating correspondence. Most recent project is assisting with development of user manuals. Test manuals and provide notes to software designers so that they can implement changes.

6/99 to 5/05, Executive Secretary ❖ **New World Packaging**

Responsible for clerical and receptionist duties for packaging firm. Maintained all office files and records. Produced correspondence. Directed all incoming calls and provided basic customer service.

❖ SKILLS ❖

Microsoft Word, Excel and PowerPoint
Typing speed of 70 wpm
Ten-key calculator by touch
Some knowledge of Spanish

❖ REFERENCES AVAILABLE ❖

JENNIFER HERNANDEZ

3125 Cool Creek Dr.

Carmel, IN 46032

(317) 555-9406

jhernandez@xxx.com

OBJECTIVE

To obtain a position as an engineer with the opportunity to apply my knowledge of digital circuit design, programmable controllers, and microprocessors.

EMPLOYMENT

Systems Engineer, July 2003-Present
Allied Wholesale Electrical Supply, Inc. ■ Indianapolis, IN

Responsibilities include:

- Resolving computer problems
- Keeping inventory
- Working with programmable controllers
- Working with CAD
- Analyzing change requests
- Writing troubleshooting documentation

Die Detailer, August 1999-June 2003
Webber Engineering ■ Carmel, IN

Responsibilities included:

- Drawing and dimensioning die details
- Making engineering changes to die drawings
- Running blueprints

EDUCATION

Lawrence Institute of Technology, Southfield, MI
B.S., Electrical Engineering, 2003
■ Passed Professional Engineering Exam, June 2005

References will be provided upon request.

Chapter 6

Sample Cover Letters

This chapter contains sample cover letters for people pursuing a wide variety of jobs and careers in scientific and technical fields or who already have experience in the field.

There are many different styles of cover letters in terms of layout, level of formality, and presentation of information. These samples also represent people with varying amounts of education and work experience. Choose one cover letter or borrow elements from several different cover letters to help you construct your own.

LEE KING

300 North Lake Shore Drive, #22

Chicago, IL 60603

June 15, 2009

ENVIRON Management
300 Butterfield Road
Oak Brook, IL 60521

Dear Personnel Director:

I am seeking a position with your firm that utilizes my training in the environmental field. I am eager to work for a firm such as ENVIRON that is implementing the latest environmental advancements and technology.

I recently earned a Bachelor of Science degree in Environmental Health Science from Indiana University. Through two paid internships with county health departments, I have participated in health and safety training, regulatory compliance, and on-site inspections.

In addition, I am an experienced technical writer and am proficient in several computer programs, including Excel, PowerPoint, and Word. During college, I was a member of several organizations, including Sigma Alpha Epsilon fraternity, the Environmental Health Association, and the Bicycling Club.

I would be delighted to meet with you at your convenience to discuss career opportunities with your firm. I can be contacted by telephone at (312) 555-8961 or email at lee.king@xxx.com.

Sincerely,

Lee King

Enclosure: Resume

Jason Dean

May 3, 2007

489 Sutton Street
New York, NY 10028
j.dean@xxx.com
(212) 555-9085

Ms. Linda Appleton
Overseas Trading Company
25 Sixth Avenue
New York, NY 10013

Dear Ms. Appleton:

I am writing concerning possible employment opportunities with your firm. In particular, I am looking for a senior MIS management position in a progressive international firm. By way of introduction, I have enclosed my resume.

As an MIS professional, I have had more than 15 years' experience developing large commercial systems. I possess a solid technical background in multi-language programming and systems design with extensive user interfacing.

Furthermore, I have direct experience in designing and establishing a systems programming organization for Deloitte & Touche to enhance the firm's internal business system. I would welcome the opportunity to assist in the enhancement of Overseas Trading Company's information systems.

I would appreciate an opportunity to discuss my background with you in greater detail. Please feel free to contact me via e-mail or phone if you would like to set up an interview at your convenience. I look forward to hearing from you.

Sincerely,

Jason Dean

Enclosure

Diane Sanchez

5958 Ivy Drive ❖ Newark, NJ 07430
(201) 555-5297 ❖ Diane.Sanchez@xxx.com

April 23, 2006

Mr. Sam Palmer
Personnel Director
Michigan Engineering
P.O. Box 250
Detroit, MI 48226

Dear Mr. Palmer:

The purpose of this letter is to ask for your firm's consideration for an available position as a Senior Industrial Engineer.

I have approximately 15 years' experience in industrial engineering and manufacturing process engineering, with an emphasis on cost and manpower reductions, general floor troubleshooting, automation, equipment justification, and line balancing.

After you have reviewed my resume, I would appreciate the opportunity to discuss with you any industrial engineering openings. I could be available to travel to Michigan for a personal interview with a week's notice. Thank you for your time and consideration.

I look forward to your response.

Sincerely,

Diane Sanchez

Enclosure

KAREN S. ADAMS

1685 Mountain Road • Tucson, AZ 85720 • Karen.Adams@xxx.com • (602) 555-8960

February 3, 2008

Rita Long, Director of Human Services

Bechtel Laboratories

488 Industrial Parkway

San Francisco, CA 94105

Dear Ms. Long:

A colleague of mine recently informed me that Bechtel is expanding and seeking applicants for numerous positions for the upcoming year. Presently I am the project coordinator for the University of Arizona Physical Plant and I'm planning to relocate to San Francisco at the end of the month. My responsibilities include such duties as managing multiple construction projects, estimating, surveying, and supervising jobs.

I am currently seeking a more demanding position with an international construction firm. My goal is to advance to a construction management position that focuses on achieving environmental compatibility in all projects undertaken. I have extensive experience coordinating and supervising multiple teams of people on high-level, long-term projects.

My resume is enclosed for your review. I would appreciate the opportunity to discuss my qualifications in detail and share my portfolio with you. I think you will agree that my skills could be an asset to Bechtel. Thank you for your time and consideration.

Sincerely,

Karen S. Adams

Enclosure

Mark F. Fulton

Current Address: Mark.Fulton@xxx.com
78 Prairie Road   Permanent Address:
Columbus, Ohio 43216   26 Frenwood Road
(614) 555-3981   Steubenville, Ohio 40605
                                    (614) 555-1807

October 9, 2007

Columbus Engineering
200 East Sixteenth Street
Columbus, Ohio 43216

Dear Mr. Hong:

I am interested in interviewing with you for an entry-level civil engineering
position.

Recently, I received my MS in Civil Engineering from the Ohio State University.
Furthermore, I recently passed the Engineer-in-Training Examination in April.

While my work experience has been primarily in the structural analysis and
design of bridges, roadways, and sewer systems, I am willing to consider
positions in other related areas.

I have enclosed my resume for your review and consideration. I would appreciate
the opportunity to meet with you personally to further discuss my qualifications. I
will follow up this letter with a telephone call in a few days.

Sincerely,

Mark F. Fulton

Enclosure

Fred Stevens

474 Drury Lane

Denver, CO 80156

(303) 555-3061

April 5, 2008

Mr. Richard Fraser
Western Telecom
3200 Valley Way
Englewood, CO 80111

Dear Mr. Fraser:

I am writing to obtain further information regarding employment opportunities with your corporation in the area of telecommunications research and development. Specifically, I am interested in pursuing a career in optical fiber networks, satellite communication, or antenna design.

I will be graduating from Denver University in June with a master's degree in Electrical Engineering. My studies have been concentrated in telecommunications and fiber optics. In addition, my summer internship enabled me to conduct research on privacy and security issues in home networks.

I have included my resume and references for your evaluation. Please feel free to contact me if you have any questions or would like to set up a time to meet. Thank you for your consideration.

Sincerely,

Fred Stevens

Enclosure

L A T I S H A   B R O W N

3300 Westwood Drive ■ Cuyahoga Falls, OH 44221

(216) 555-6929 ■ Latisha.Brown@xxx.com

June 15, 2009

Mr. Victor Lord, Senior Partner
Industrial Design Group, Inc.
488 West Lafayette Blvd.
Cuyahoga Falls, OH 44221

Dear Mr. Lord:

I am very interested in pursuing a designer/drafter position with
Industrial Design Group, Inc. A copy of my resume is enclosed for your
review.

Through my present employment with Commercial Design, I have refined
my design and detail skills. My work with this firm entails design
development of mechanical, electrical, and plumbing systems for major
commercial projects. I have gained firsthand experience with developing
the construction details of the engineering and architectural concepts, as
well as preparing the final bid documentation.

I look forward to hearing from you soon to further discuss my
qualifications.

Sincerely,

Latisha Brown

Enclosure

Evan Lindquist

6189 Beach Road, #9C

Jacksonville, FL 32209

904-555-1263

April 15, 2007

Jack Castillo
General Aeronautics
100 Canaveral Road
Daytona Beach, FL 32014

Dear Mr. Castillo:

This letter is in response to your advertisement in last Tuesday's *Miami Herald*. I am interested in the aerospace engineer position with your firm.

Currently I am working as a Strength Engineer for Aerospace International, where I am responsible for conducting detailed stress analysis for aircraft engine components. Previously, I was a Value Engineer with Aircraft Technology Corporation, working on aircraft air-conditioning systems, and a Stress Engineer with Goddard Aerospace Systems, working on various commercial aircraft. Based on my experience, I believe that I could make a valuable contribution to General Aeronautics.

I hope to further discuss my qualifications with you in an interview.

Yours truly,

Evan Lindquist

Enclosure

Scott Monroe

64 Fountain Lake Road   Gary, IN 46408   (219) 555-6823
scott.monroe@xxx.com

May 28, 2008

Mr. Tony Cruciano
Carnegie Steel
Gary, IN 46408

Dear Mr. Cruciano:

I wish to apply for a position as a Technology Manager with Carnegie Steel.
I currently possess bachelor's and master's degrees in Information and
Global Technology Management. In addition, I have worked for more than
eighteen years as a steelmaking reliability supervisor and manager and as a
steel operations maintenance engineer. I believe that my education coupled
with my extensive experience could be of value to your firm.

My areas of expertise include:

- International issues in electronic commerce
- Managing Internet infrastructure
- Enterprise Resource Planning (ERP)
- Supply Chain Management (SCM)
- Customer Resource Management (CRM)
- Societal impacts of IT in developing countries

For your review, I am enclosing my resume. Please feel free to reach me by
phone or email at (219) 555-6823 or scott.monroe@xxx.com.

Sincerely yours,

Scott Monroe
Enclosure: Resume

Rachel Schwartzman

125 College Way
Princeton, NJ 08545
Email: schwartz@xxx.com
Cellular: (609) 555-7854

March 30, 2008

Sandia Robotics
Human Resources
500 East 29th Street
Mobile, AL 36601

SUBJECT: Opening in robotics lab for a programmer

To whom it may concern:

I am writing to you with the hope that you might have an opening soon in your robotics laboratory for a programmer. If you do not, I would appreciate your keeping my resume on file for upcoming opportunities.

My coursework for a bachelor's degree in mechanical engineering will be completed in June 2007 from Princeton University. Currently, I am performing independent robotics research on the use of linear motor robots in assembly as a result of my research fellowship.

People who know me well consider me to be dedicated, hardworking, and creative. I enjoy challenging work and perform well under pressure. I believe that these characteristics fit with the type of professional you will be seeking.

Thank you for considering my qualifications. I look forward to hearing from you soon.

Sincerely,

Rachel Schwartzman

Enclosure

PATRICIA GOLDBERG

1480 Dean Road ■ Sacramento, CA 95819 ■ Patty.Goldberg@xxx.com ■ (916) 555-9306

March 30, 2009

Ms. Consuelo Flores
EnviroTek
33 Sierra Road
Los Angeles, CA 90024

Dear Ms. Flores:

For almost ten years, I have pursued a satisfying career with the California Department of Environmental Management. At this point in my career, I would like to make a change to the private sector.

During my career, I have held positions as an Environmental Project Manager, State Cleanup Section; an Environmental Manager, Facilities Planning Section; and as an Environmental Scientist, Permits Section. My responsibilities have included managing the cleanup of hazardous waste sites, reviewing construction plans for water treatment facilities, and writing municipal permits. As a result, I have become more adept at maneuvering through the bureaucracy to make things happen quickly.

I would welcome the opportunity to speak with you about my background and the potential areas where my expertise could be best utilized by your firm. A resume is enclosed detailing my qualifications.

Sincerely,

Patricia Goldberg

Enclosure: Resume

BRYAN PULLMAN

43 Buffalo Bill Road   Omaha, NE 68129   (402) 555-5837   B.Pullman@xxx.com

September 27, 2007

Star Tribune
P.O. Box 744
Houston, TX 77022

SUBJECT: Opening for project geologist

I am sending my resume in response to Wednesday's ad for a project geologist. I am interested in relocating to the Houston area and would be available to relocate with two weeks' notice. As you can see from my resume, I have more than four years of experience in managing environmental assessments as well as designing groundwater recovery and treatment systems.

I would like to meet with you to discuss my qualifications and background. I believe that I would be a productive addition to your engineering staff. Thank you for your consideration.

Sincerely,

Bryan Pullman

Enclosure

JOHN K. LAI

20 West Concord Street   Dover, NH 03820   John.Lai@xxx.com   (603) 555-1703

October 8, 2007

Ms. Millicent Jones
Hancock Construction
1501 Pennsylvania Ave., NW
Washington, D.C. 20006

Dear Ms. Jones:

I am writing to follow up our telephone conversation of yesterday morning regarding Hancock Construction's need for a project manager in Beijing. As we discussed, I am currently wrapping up a construction project for Johnson, Incorporated, and am seeking a project management position overseas. My work experience combined with my fluency in Mandarin Chinese uniquely qualifies me for this position.

I will be available for employment at the start of the new year. Also, short-term relocation to Beijing presents no problems for my family.

I have enclosed my resume and references as you requested. I'm looking forward to discussing the position further during our phone interview on October 12th at 1 PM ET. If you have any questions in the meantime, please feel free to contact me via phone or email.

Sincerely,

John K. Lai

Enclosure

EDGAR PETERS

9 De Soot Drive
Baton Rouge, Louisiana 70805
edgar.peters@xxx.com
(504) 555-1388

July 13, 2008

Southern Glassworks
350 Florida Street
New Orleans, LA 70112

Dear Personnel Manager:

This letter is in response to Sunday's advertisement in the *New Orleans Picayune* for an industrial engineer. Please accept my resume in consideration for this position.

With a master's degree in industrial engineering from Tulane University and five years of work experience as an industrial engineer at Alexander Steel Company, I believe that I'm well-suited to your company's needs.

Thank you for your time. I look forward to hearing from you soon regarding the position at Southern Glassworks.

Sincerely,

Edgar Peters

Enclosure

Steven R. Kohlhase

473 Hill Drive
Kenosha, WI 53143
steve.kohlhase@xxx.com
(414) 555-6320

June 17, 2007

Mr. Richard Serafini
Alistates Engineering
6341 Crestwood Drive, Suite 416
Naperville, IL 60665

Dear Mr. Serafini:

Given your company's excellent reputation in environmental engineering, hydrogeology, and solid waste, your firm must appreciate the need for polished, professional business writing for all the project reports you submit. My education in environmental science and work experience as a technical writer and editor with an engineering firm have given me the knowledge and solid writing skills that can benefit a firm like yours.

My enclosed resume will show you that I have a good background in public affairs. As you will also notice, my coursework in environmental chemistry, geology, and systems analysis have provided a strong foundation for my career focus on environmental writing. I am also very familiar with reading blueprints, reviewing cost estimates, change orders, and bidding procedures. I work well under pressure and have consistently met publishing deadlines. In addition, I am a skilled electronics technician.

Because proven ability and skills are best evaluated in person, I would appreciate an interview with you. Thank you for your time and your consideration.

Respectfully yours,

Steven R. Kohlhase

Enclosure

Gordon Extine

2556 Broadlawn Street
Houston, TX 88674
gordonextine@xxx.com

May 27, 2008

Personnel Director
Dimetrics, Inc.
P.O. Box 788964
San Francisco, CA 94147

Greetings:

I would like to be considered for an environmental position with Dimetrics, Inc. I have graduated from Notre Dame with a B.S. in Public Affairs. My majors were Environmental Science and Environmental Affairs.

I feel that my experience in the field of environmental science and as student assistant to the science department, along with my education, qualifies me for a position with your firm. I enjoy challenges and hard work and am concerned with doing the best that I can at all times.

I would like to request an interview to discuss how my placement with your firm would benefit both of us. Please phone me at (218) 555-8866. I look forward to hearing from you.

Yours truly,

Gordon Extine

Enclosure

FELICITAS A. FINNER

Telephone 415-555-9466
55778 Ventura Blvd.
Encino, CA 91319
felicitasfinner@xxx.com

July 2, 2007

Mr. David Mendoza
Director, Human Resources
Cimflex Corporation
P.O. Box 887
Topeka, KS 66608

Dear Mr. Mendoza:

Thank you for speaking to me by phone this afternoon. As you know, I am pursuing a career in robotics and would like to learn more about Cimflex Corporation.

In May of this year I graduated from Indiana University with a bachelor's degree in robotic engineering. My internship with Ecotron Engineering offered me valuable exposure to the operations of a consulting firm involved in the robotics field.

The enclosed resume should assist you in evaluating my qualifications. If you need further information, please let me know. I look forward to meeting with you to discuss employment with your company. Thank you for your consideration.

Sincerely,

Felicitas A. Finner

Enclosure

Elizabeth A. Grossa

1346 E. 22nd St., #105
Carbondale, IL 62901
(217) 555-9142
elizabethgrossa@xxx.com

May 26, 2007

Indianapolis Star
P. O. Box 279
Indianapolis, IN 46227

APPLICATION FOR STRUCTURAL ENGINEERING POSITION

This letter is in response to the ad placed in this Sunday's edition of the *Indianapolis Star.*

I will earn my B.S. degree in Structural Engineering from Southern Illinois University this August. I have specialized in the fields of structural integrity and finite elements analysis. Your ad was of particular interest to me, as the job also includes some customer and sales interaction.

Enclosed is my resume, which details my work experience and educational background. I would welcome the opportunity to meet with you to discuss my experience and qualifications.

Sincerely,

Elizabeth A. Grossa

Enclosure

DAN LUI

17 Dinge Road   Terre Haute, IN 52211

317/555-1331 (Home)   317/555-2339 (Office)   danlui@xxx.com

August 21, 2008

Farrallon, Inc.
787 E. Fourier Drive
Emeryville, CA 96998
Attn: Robert Crain, Director of Human Services

Dear Mr. Crain:

After your visit to Rose-Hulman last March, we spoke about opportunities within your company for biotech assistants. You indicated that new positions would be opening this fall. I am writing to request an interview for one of those openings.

In May, I graduated from Rose-Hulman with a B.S. in Applied Biology. I was one of fifteen out of two hundred who graduated with honors. My coursework included Evolutionary Biology, Ecology, Plant Structure and Function, and Technical Communications.

As I look forward to my career in this field, I know that I would be able to make good use of my education working for Farrallon.

I have enclosed a copy of my resume and will call next week to discuss setting up an interview.

Sincerely,

Dan Lui

Edda Fisher

■ eddafisher@xxx.com ■ (713) 555-8866

January 27, 2009

Personnel Director
Valley Hospital
P.O. Box 228964
Birmingham, AL 35222-8964

Dear Personnel Director:

Please consider my application for a position as a dietitian. I graduated from Purdue University with a Bachelor of Science degree in dietetics, and have been a registered dietitian for the past three years.

I feel that my experience as a dietitian in a nursing home and clinic, along with my education, qualifies me for a position with Valley Hospital. I enjoy the challenge of helping people regain their health through proper diet. Furthermore, I work hard and am concerned with doing my best at all times.

I would like to request an interview to discuss how my placement with your hospital would be of mutual benefit. Please phone me any time at (713) 555-8866. I look forward to hearing from you.

Yours truly,

Edda Fisher

eddafisher@xxx.com

Enclosure